75 Ways to Be a Better Teacher Tomorrow

Highly-effective teachers have something in common: They do simple things extraordinarily well—simple, uncomplicated things on a daily basis. In this new book by bestselling authors and presenters Annette Breaux and Todd Whitaker, you'll learn the secrets of these tried-and-true techniques that will help to improve your teaching, your students' learning, and your students' behavior. Annette and Todd, who have years of experience working in schools across the globe, reveal 75 easily-implemented strategies that will improve teaching, classroom management, student motivation, student achievement, parent communication, and more—with no new programs! Each tip provides practical takeaways that can be used immediately and with remarkable success.

Annette Breaux (@AnnetteBreaux) is a well-known speaker and consultant in education today. She is a former classroom teacher, curriculum coordinator, and teacher induction coordinator. She has written several bestsellers including *101 Answers for New Teachers and Their Mentors, Seven Simple Secrets: What the BEST Teachers Know and Do,* and *50 Ways to Improve Student Behavior.*

Todd Whitaker (@toddwhitaker) is a professor of educational leadership at the University of Missouri. He is a leading presenter in the field of education and has written more than 50 books including the national bestsellers *What Great Teachers Do Differently* and *Your First Year: How to Survive and Thrive as a New Teacher,* co-written with Madeline Whitaker Good and Katherine Whitaker.

75 Ways to Be a Better Teacher Tomorrow

With Less Stress and Quick Success

Annette Breaux and Todd Whitaker

Routledge
Taylor & Francis Group

NEW YORK AND LONDON

First published 2019
by Routledge
711 Third Avenue, New York, NY 10017

and by Routledge
2 Park Square, Milton Park, Abingdon, Oxon, OX14 4RN

Routledge is an imprint of the Taylor & Francis Group, an informa business

© 2019 Taylor & Francis

The rights of Annette Breaux and Todd Whitaker to be identified as
authors of this work has been asserted by them in accordance with
sections 77 and 78 of the Copyright, Designs and Patents Act 1988.

Library of Congress Cataloging-in-Publication Data
A catalog record for this title has been requested

ISBN: 978-1-138-36337-3 (hbk)
ISBN: 978-1-138-36338-0 (pbk)
ISBN: 978-0-429-43164-7 (ebk)

Typeset in Palatino
by Swales & Willis Ltd, Exeter, UK

KV 11.14.2018 0751

Contents

About the Authors

Annette Breaux is one of the most entertaining and informative authors and speakers in education today. She leaves her audiences with practical techniques to implement in their classrooms immediately. Administrators agree that they see results from teachers the next day.

Annette is a former classroom teacher, curriculum coordinator, and author of Louisiana FIRST, a statewide induction program for new teachers. Annette also served as the Teacher Induction Coordinator for Nicholls State University in Thibodaux, Louisiana. She co-authored a book with Dr. Harry K. Wong on new-teacher induction. Her other writings include: *101 Answers for New Teachers and Their Mentors*, *REAL Teachers, REAL Challenges, REAL Solutions*, *101 Poems for Teachers*, *Seven Simple Secrets: What the BEST Teachers Know and Do*, *50 Ways to Improve Student Behavior*, *Making Good Teaching Great*, *The Ten-Minute Inservice*, and *Quick Answers for Busy Teachers*.

Teachers who have read Annette's writings or heard Annette speak agree that they come away with user-friendly information, heartfelt inspiration, and a much-needed reminder that theirs is the most noble of all professions.

Dr. Todd Whitaker is a professor of educational leadership at the University of Missouri and professor emeritus at Indiana State University. He has spent his life pursuing his love of education by researching and studying effective teachers and principals.

Prior to moving into higher education, he was a math teacher and basketball coach in Missouri. Todd then served as a principal at the middle school, junior high, and high school levels. He was also a middle school coordinator in charge of staffing, curriculum, and technology for the opening of new middle schools.

One of the nation's leading authorities on staff motivation, teacher leadership, and principal effectiveness, Todd has written over 50 books including the national best seller *What Great Teachers Do Differently*. Other titles include: *Dealing With Difficult Teachers, The Ten-Minute Inservice, Your First Year, What Great Principals Do Differently, Motivating & Inspiring Teachers,* and *Dealing With Difficult Parents.*

Twitter: @AnnetteBreaux and @ToddWhitaker

Preface

Highly-effective teachers have something in common: They do simple things extraordinarily well—simple, uncomplicated things on a daily basis. They don't strive to be perfect, but they do strive to be just a little better each day. They are realistic enough to know that teaching can be difficult, overwhelming, time-consuming, and exhausting. But they are also realistic enough to know that they can only do so much on any given day. They accept this, they embrace it, they recognize that they can and do make a difference in the lives of their students, they don't stress over things that are outside of their control, and they continue to do the simple things that keep them ahead of the pack.

Our purpose for writing this book is to share some of the tried-and-true, simple techniques used by highly-effective teachers. Notice that none of these techniques and activities are difficult. Most occur during class time. They require no studying and no practice at all. They are designed to help you to become more efficient and effective, accomplishing more in less time. You can implement any of them immediately and see results instantly, all while having fun!

How to Use This Book

This book lends itself to four groups of educators:

1. **Teachers**: If you're seeking to improve your skills and improve student achievement and behavior, then this book is for you. Try one tip at a time, and choose the ones you feel are most relevant and appropriate for you and your classroom situation. You may also choose to use the book during meetings with your professional learning communities. Discuss specific tips, go back to your classrooms to try them, and return to your groups with feedback as to how you implemented them and how your students reacted.

2. **Mentors**: Share any and all of the ideas to help new teachers ease into the profession in a way that will not overwhelm them but rather will help them to experience immediate success. Pick and choose which tips you choose to share and when you choose to share them. This may vary from teacher to teacher, but all new teachers can benefit from all tips in the book.

3. **Administrators:** This book is perfect for sharing ideas at faculty meetings. Take one tip and hold a group discussion about it. Then send everyone back to their classrooms to give it a try. You might also choose to use specific tips when meeting with certain teachers—to provide suggestions for improvement in specific areas.

4. **Staff Development Professionals:** Each tip can serve as a mini-inservice when you are training teachers. Or you may choose to use several at a time. However you choose to use them, the book provides 75 ways to help teachers improve teaching, learning, and student behavior!

Five Things This Book Will Do for You

1. Improve your effectiveness in the classroom
2. Improve your efficiency in the classroom
3. Make teaching more enjoyable
4. Provide insight into what separates the best teachers from all the rest
5. Help you to be the kind of teacher students love, respect, and work for

Five Things This Book Will NOT Do for You

1. Overwhelm you
2. Eat away at your precious time
3. Make you a perfect teacher or make your students perfect students. It will, however, make you a better teacher with better-behaved and better-performing students. So, you won't be a perfect teacher when you finish this book, even if you implement every suggestion. But you will be a better teacher, even if you implement only one!
4. Promote any programs, fads, or trends in education. Rather, the techniques will work with ANY program, fad, or trend in education.
5. Add to your workload. (If anything, it will lessen both your burden and your workload by helping you to be more efficient and more effective!)

Reminder

Go easy on yourself. Don't try all 75 at once. If you implement even one of these, you'll be a better teacher. If you implement two, you'll be even better. And if you eventually implement all 75, you'll be downright dangerous! Do what the best teachers do: Take small, consistent steps toward improvement. Do your best, then rest. Lather, rinse, repeat.

Enjoy!

Swallow Negative Words

What to Do

Wager a bet with a coworker. Whoever can go the longest without speaking negatively to or about a student (or anything education-related) gets treated to dinner by the loser. (Well, what if you both go for three whole weeks without saying or doing anything negative? Then the principal ought to treat you *both* to dinner!)

How and Why to Do It

Select a willing teacher with whom to wager this bet. But don't just pick any teacher. Obviously, you don't want to partner with the most positive teacher in the school. You're doomed to be picking up the tab. If you partner with the most negative teacher, it's an easy win, right? Yes, hopefully for both of you. Maybe they can't go longer than two days without faltering. But for those two days, that person is a better teacher. That's a plus for the teacher and the students. The plus for you is that you also go for at least two days without faltering *and* are now the recipient of a free meal! You may, however, want to accept a bit more of a challenge by partnering with someone who falls somewhere between the most positive and most negative teacher. It's up to you! The important thing is that you actually do it, because it's no secret that positive teachers are inherently better than negative ones. Both can be found on any campus.

Notice that this little "game" takes no extra time, no extra learning/studying, and no practice. It takes the same amount of time to be positive as it does to be negative. But negative thinking takes a toll on everyone around. Negativity can bring us down, both in mood and performance. Resist its temptations. Students want and deserve positive role models. Every time you're just a little nicer and a little more positive, you're a lot more effective! In the words of Winston Churchill, "By swallowing evil words unsaid, no one has ever harmed his stomach."

What's to stop you from wagering more of the same bet with other teachers? Hey, you could be eating lots of free meals if you play your cards right! You could also be changing the culture of your school, one teacher at a time.

2

Ask Yourself Five Questions

What to Do

Today, you'll be doing a quick self-assessment consisting of five simple questions. Do this alone, and don't share the results with anyone. Your honest answers to these five questions can change the way you teach, tomorrow!

How and Why to Do It

Here are five questions to which highly-effective teachers work hard to answer YES.

1. Do the students know I care about each of them? (Students who doubt this are almost always causing problems in the classroom.)
2. Do my students think that I am on their side? (Being "on their side" does not mean that you take their side even if they are misbehaving. It means you care about them, you support them, and you

genuinely want what's best for them. They need to know this, but we often neglect to convince them.)

3. Do my students think that I *love* teaching?
4. Do my students feel that they can succeed in my class? (A student who feels he/she can't be successful will give up. Giving up leads to obvious problems.)
5. Do I do all I can to make learning fun and interesting in my class?

Let's say that you found one or two areas that may require a little attention on your part. What's most important is that you are aware of these. You have to be *aware* in order to *improve*. So, if you're not sure if the students know that you love teaching (and they have to think this in order for you to get their best from them), then *tell* them that you love teaching. Tell them why. And start acting more as though you love teaching. Remember, one step at a time. Small bites. You can do this during class time, and it literally takes no skill or practice. It only takes a commitment from you to eventually answer "yes" to all five questions.

3

Make One Lesson
More Fun!

What to Do

Take one lesson you were already planning to teach. Do a quick online search for a fun activity to go with that lesson. Find just one idea and use it in the place of something "less fun" that you were going to do.

How and Why to Do It

Let's say that you're about to teach a lesson on pronouns. Okay, so we all know that pronouns take the place of nouns. Not very exciting, is it? You were planning to introduce a list of pronouns—I, she, he, we, they, them, and so on—and then you were going to assign some written exercises where students identify pronouns and explain which nouns those pronouns are replacing. How fun is that?

Instead, you do a five-minute online search and find a great idea—one that's simple, easy, and fun. You give your students a list of pronouns and have them write three sentences about themselves and something they love to do. The key is that they cannot use any of the words in the list—no pronouns. Then they share their sentences with the class. So Hank reads his: "Hank likes to shoot hoops with Hank's friends. Hank and Hank's friends get together almost every day after school at the park and Hank and Hank's friends play against other kids." And another example: Keisha likes to draw. Keisha is taking art lessons and Keisha's teacher is putting Keisha in the art show next weekend.

The student's love this because their sentences sound weird, long, and awkward. Bingo! Pronouns make a language more efficient and less awkward. Most people don't know this. They know *how* to use pronouns, but they never stopped to think about *why* we use them.

For a fun homework assignment, have the students go home and speak to a family member without using pronouns. It takes about ten seconds for the family member to look at them like they're crazy. Tomorrow, they will share with the class how their family reacted to them. Students actually *do* this type of homework, because it's fun!

When you teach this way, students learn more in less time and have fun doing it. Win!

4

Learn One Important Thing About Each Student

What to Do

Your goal today is simple: Learn *one* important thing about each student. It can be one thing they like, one thing that motivates them, one thing they're good at, etc. The key is to focus on one thing. Don't try to learn everything—that can be overwhelming and impossible. Focus on one. NOTE: If you teach at the secondary level and have multiple classes, you may want to do this one class at a time in order to make it more manageable.

How and Why to Do It

Tell your students you love getting to know as much about them as you can. Have them write a sentence or two about either something they enjoy doing or just something they would like for you to know about them that you may not already know. This only takes a couple of minutes.

After collecting these, be sure to read each and begin to use the information to help you cement a positive relationship with your students. If Wendell says he likes to play guitar, ask him about it. Heck, let him bring his guitar to school and play a song for the class if he's willing. What's important is that you take an interest. It takes no extra time out of your day. Wendell is in your class each day. As he enters your room, ask, "How's the guitar playing going?" "Sarah, did you see any good movies this weekend?" "Joe, how many miles did you run this week?" You get the point.

It's important to be prepared for students' responses. They're not always positive. A student may say, "I live with my grandmother because my mom is in jail." That's an important piece of information that you can use in developing a trusting relationship with that student.

So how can this simple, two-minute activity help to make you a better teacher tomorrow? Because students behave better and work harder for people who care about them and make them feel like they matter. Be prepared to read that sentence again throughout the book because it cannot be stressed enough. *Students behave better and work harder for people who care about them and make them feel like they matter!*

5

Change the Expression on Your Face

What to Do

Smile. That's it? Smile? Yes, smile. Most teachers, if asked, will admit that they do not smile most of the time in the classroom. They appear far too serious. Some look down-right mad. We're not suggesting that most teachers never smile. They just don't smile enough. But highly-effective teachers know a secret. If you simply change the expression on your face to a smile, and you keep that expression on your face all day long, you get incredibly positive results instantly!

How and Why to Do It

All the while you wear a smile, endorphins race through your brain.
But turn it upside down to a frown, and everyone's now in pain.

Frowning ages you, and it ages everyone around you. It is exhausting to be negative or to be in the company of someone who is negative. On the flipside, it's uplifting to be around someone who is positive. And when you smile, your brain releases endorphins making you feel happy—even if that smile is *fake*!

Try it for one day. Just one. Simply smile all day in your classroom. Okay, so if a student misbehaves, you probably won't be smiling at him/her. But you will see less of these instances when you are smiling. What's the downside to smiling? There is none. What's the upside? You and your students will be happier and more productive.

For now, try it for one day. Just one. There's science behind this, really. It's free, it takes no extra time, and it yields positive results. Students like teachers who appear happy. When students like you, they're more likely to learn from you. And once you see the results, you're much more likely to make this a daily habit. As a bonus, if you're someone who doesn't typically smile all day, it's fun to watch your students' reactions when you *do* smile all day!

6

Leave One Compliment a Day

What to Do

Get a stuffed animal and make it the class mascot. This animal will begin delivering one compliment a day to a student. As students arrive, the mascot will be inside of one student's desk. Attached to it will be a compliment about that particular student.

How and Why to Do It

Name the stuffed animal. Tell students that "Bubba the Bear" (just an example—pick your own name and animal or feel free to use ours) will be watching every day and deciding whose desk he wants to sleep in each night. And before you're tempted to think that this is geared toward elementary students only, we should tell you we stole this idea from a high school teacher. We've since shared it and have seen it used successfully at all grade levels. For older students, you may even want to use a miniature version of the school's mascot.

During today's lesson, decide who will be tomorrow's recipient for that particular class. As you walk around the room helping students, jot a one-sentence compliment about a deserving student. Don't do this after class or after school, because this will add to your already-busy day. If you decide to leave it in Carlos' desk tomorrow, jot a compliment down today. "I noticed that you've been paying attention better in class. Congrats!" When Carlos gets to school tomorrow and sees Bubba and a compliment in his desk, guess what he's even more likely to do for the day? Pay attention better. If you don't believe that students of all ages love to receive a compliment attached to a stuffed animal in their desk, you've obviously never tried it!

Notice how worn and tattered that stuffed animal soon becomes, and notice how excited the students are (even though some will pretend it's ridiculous) to see that stuffed animal in their desk when they arrive. We have yet to encounter a student who doesn't read the compliment!

7

Ask for Student Feedback on a Lesson

What to Do

Following one of your lessons today, elicit feedback from the students—what they did/did not like and what you could have possibly done better.

How and Why to Do It

This is a very easy activity that can lead to improvement in your teaching tomorrow. Yet, most teachers admit that they rarely do this. We're not suggesting that you do this for every lesson. We're just asking you to try it for one!

After a lesson, ask students, "How could I have taught that lesson better?" Tell them what you were hoping to accomplish, and then ask how you could have helped them to achieve the lesson's goal better. Let them think about it and then write their responses, anonymously. Read each, respond to the students, telling them which ideas you intend to use in future lessons, and then use at least one of those suggestions to improve your next lesson.

A teacher recently shared that he asked this of his students and was amazed by the helpful suggestions. "My students suggested ideas for activities that would have definitely involved and engaged them more and would have been more fun, interesting, and motivating for all of us. I'm going to continue asking for suggestions!"

What do you accomplish by simply asking for student feedback about your lesson? You enable them to actually think about *what* they just learned and *how* they learned it. You let them know that their ideas are valued. You show that you are open to their suggestions. You give the message that they matter to you and that their success is important to you. But the biggest win is for you in that you receive useful feedback for improving your teaching.

Reflecting on their careers, most retired teachers will say that the students, undoubtedly, were always their greatest teachers. Don't wait until you retire to use that fact to benefit *your* teaching and *their* learning!

8

Assign Two Purposes to Your Desk

What to Do

Look at that piece of furniture in your classroom known as "the teacher's desk" and assign the following two purposes to it: (1) To be used to do your paperwork/planning when the students are not present, and (2) To hold some of your stuff.

How and Why to Do It

The two purposes stated above are the only two reasons we even have such a thing as a desk. We don't have a desk to sit behind when students are working. We don't have a desk to sit behind during student or parent conferences. We don't have a desk for doing work while our students are in the room. And the chair behind it is not for resting while the students are present. If you really do need to take a load off of your feet for a few minutes, get a rolling chair and roll around from student desk to student desk or from group to group. Place the chair in the middle of the students during a discussion. This way, you're still "with" the students as opposed to being separated from them.

Physical barriers between teachers and students create mental barriers between teachers and students. Have you ever seen a coach giving a motivational speech or teaching players a new skill from behind a desk? It's not possible to be effective when you are behind a desk. During conferences with students or parents, sit beside the person. Sitting beside someone conveys that you're in this "with" them. Sitting across your desk from someone conveys that you just might be against them.

Do use that desk to do your planning, grading, etc. before school, after school, or during your planning period. And *do* use it to hold some of your stuff. (The reason we say "some" of your stuff is that teachers have way too much stuff to be held by one desk!)

Any principal will tell you that it just doesn't look right when you walk into a classroom and see a teacher seated behind the desk. Invariably, that teacher jumps up. No one is fooled by this. So, just make sure that you don't put yourself in that position, literally or figuratively. Teachers who are actively engaged with the students accomplish far more than those who can often be found seated behind their desks. Plus, you burn more calories when you're moving!

9

Greet Every Student Every Day

What to Do

Greet your students every day, and act as though you are elated to see them. Fake it if you must. Say goodbye to each student every day and act as though you can't wait to see them again tomorrow. Again, fake it if you must.

How and Why to Do It

Some teachers are greeters, and others are more akin to cattle herders. The latter group hurries students into the room each day. They don't appear overly enthusiastic. Some days, they don't appear enthusiastic at all. Thus, the students appear less than enthusiastic as they enter the room and even less enthusiastic when they exit the room.

Highly-effective teachers know a secret: If you want your students to act enthusiastically, *you* have to appear enthusiastic first. And the best time to start is the second each student enters the room.

Here's all you need to do: Stand at the door with a huge smile on your face as the students enter your room. Give them a fist bump, high five, or handshake and say hello to each student. Even on days when you don't feel it, appear elated to see them—"How are you?" "Good to see you!" "Thanks for coming to class." "Glad you're back. Hope you're feeling better." And when they leave, stand at the door and tell each goodbye. Remember to act as though you can't wait to see them tomorrow.

This one simple gesture may be one of the biggest game-changers in education. It's so simple, it takes no extra time out of your day, it's completely free, and it sets the mood for a productive class period. So why aren't all teachers doing this?

When students feel like you want them in your classroom and that you're happy to see them, they're more likely to want to come to class and to want to do their best. We work harder for people who value us. Period.

Help Students to Follow Instructions

What to Do

Today, when you give instructions for an activity, give the instructions at least twice (preferably three times)—in different ways. It adds about 30 seconds to the front end of the lesson and can save precious minutes during the activity!

How and Why to Do It

We've all been there. We give instructions, very clearly. All eyes are on us, so we assume the students are listening. Then, as soon as we tell them to get busy, three things happen: (1) A few students get busy, just as you instructed, (2) Several students begin asking their neighbors what to do, and (3) Some don't even ask. They just stare blankly into nothingness. So what do we do? First, we become flustered. Second, we show that we are flustered. And then we reluctantly repeat the directions, usually in the same way that we said it the first time.

Starting today, give instructions at least twice, if not three times, and in different ways. It's easy, it's free, it helps ensure that the students all understand what to do, and it saves your sanity!

Example: Let's say you are doing a quick review, and you want to get feedback in order to check for understanding. Say, "I'm going to call out some review questions in a yes/no format. If the answer is yes, give me a thumbs-up. And if the answer is no, give me a thumbs-down." (Demonstrate while you tell them.) Part two: Say, "Now tell me what you will do if the answer is yes. (Students answer.) If the answer is no..." (Students answer.) Part three: "This time, don't tell me but show me. What will you do if the answer is yes?" (Students show you.) "If the answer is no?" (Students show you.)

Now, everyone is clear about what to do. And notice that you didn't just repeat the instructions three times. Instead, you *told* and *showed* them. Then you asked them to *tell* you. Then you asked them to *show* you. Now everyone is clear and your sanity in intact! Easy breezy!

11

Never Miss a Birthday

What to Do

This simple act—acknowledging the birthday of each student—is an act of kindness, an act of acknowledgment of the importance of the day a student entered this world, and an act of celebration that the student exists. Don't miss this simple opportunity!

How and Why to Do It

Do a quick online search for a "printable birthday calendar." Pick one, print it, and put it on your classroom wall. Have each student take ten seconds to write their name on the calendar on the date of their birthday. Next, print some free online birthday cards. Decide on a special "gift" that you will give students on their birthdays. Make it a free gift—a homework pass, a "sit at the teacher's desk" pass, etc.

Finally, have a plan for what it will look like when a student enters the room on his birthday. Let's say that today is John's birthday. As he walks into the room, you will already be at the door greeting students. Put a paper crown on his head or a sticker on his hand and wish him a happy birthday. When he gets to his desk, he will see a card from you along with a gift (like one we just suggested). And as soon as you start class, mention his birthday and have everyone sing to him. He can wear his crown and/or sticker or not. It's up to him. He can act embarrassed while everyone sings to him. That's fine. Even adults go to restaurants on their birthdays and risk being sung to by the staff in the presence of everyone in the restaurant.

Don't neglect celebrating student birthdays that fall on weekends, holidays, or summer months. Choose to celebrate those any way you'd like and at any time you'd like. Just don't forget to do it! We never get too old to appreciate being made to feel special. High school students appreciate it every bit as much as first-graders!

So how does acknowledging student birthdays make you a better teacher? It's simple: Such an act of kindness from a teacher earns students' respect, trust, and admiration. In classrooms where students respect, trust, and admire their teachers, they give better efforts to both their studies and their behavior.

12

Invite an Administrator to Your Room

What to Do

Go to one of your administrators and invite him or her to your room with the express purpose of providing useful, informal feedback that will help you to improve. Highly-effective teachers do this regularly. You'll soon see why.

How and Why to Do It

Go to your principal or assistant principal and ask,

> Could you spare about 20 minutes this week to come and observe me informally? I'm always trying to improve, and I've been working on a couple of techniques I'd love for you to observe so that you can give me some feedback.

No competent administrator will turn down a teacher who actively seeks help, feedback, and advice. All administrators want their teachers to be better because when the teacher improves, the students improve. And when the teachers and students are improving, the school is improving!

Schedule a specific time so that you will not feel pressured. Tell your administrator what you would like him/her to observe. For instance,

> I've been working on improving student engagement. I have a new activity that I'm implementing where I pair students during class discussions and then have each pair provide ongoing feedback to the entire class. I'd love for you to see this in action and let me know what you think. I'd also love to hear any suggestions you may have to help me improve student engagement even more. What would be a good day and time for you?

Why is doing this important, and how will it help you to improve? *By inviting an administrator into your classroom and asking for feedback, you accomplish several things*:

◆ You show that you are a dedicated teacher who seeks ongoing improvement.
◆ You challenge yourself to step outside of your comfort zone.
◆ You receive feedback without the pressures of formal evaluation, and
◆ You shock your administrators because they rarely get *asked* to come in and observe!

13

Don't Take Student Behavior Personally

What to Do

Our simple tip for today is this: Do not take student behavior personally.

This one is not at all difficult, but it may require a readjustment of your current way of thinking.

How and Why to Do It

How can a teacher listen to a student who is acting disrespectfully toward that teacher and not take it personally? How can a teacher witness a student's constant eye rolls and sighs and not take it personally? How can a teacher see a student continue to put forth little to no effort in class and not take it personally? How can a teacher overhear a student speaking negatively about that teacher and not take it personally?

Here's how highly-effective teachers manage to avoid taking student behavior personally:

1. They remind themselves, daily, that their students are fighting their own personal battles. Sometimes, little kids are fighting adult-level battles in their personal lives. You just never know.
2. They tell themselves, "It's not me. I just happen to be the nearest adult to you at this moment. I'll remember that and remember to act like an adult when dealing with you."
3. They ask questions instead of attacking the student. "I can tell you're really upset right now. Are you okay? Do you need to talk about it? If so, I'm here for you."

These teachers do not simply look the other way while a student is obviously in distress. Instead, they give the student time and space to calm down and then they speak with the student privately. Are there ever consequences for the students regarding their actions? Sure. But those consequences are appropriate, well thought-out, and never given as a result of the teacher's hurt feelings.

Let's say that you really try not to take student behavior personally, yet you do experience hurt feelings when a student acts a certain way in your presence. Then practice your skill of "faking it." Pretend you're not personally offended, and act accordingly. A student will respond differently (in a more positive way) to a teacher who does not take his behavior personally—one who truly does attack the problem and not the person.

14

Say Three Nice Things to the Student Who Aggravates You Most

What to Do

Today, select one student—the one who aggravates you most and can threaten your sanity more than any other student. Say three nice things to that student. We'll show you how.

How and Why to Do It

We all have that one student—the one who leans on your last nerve, who threatens your mental stability, and who is, frankly, difficult to like. What typically happens is that this type of student gets "rewarded" when the teacher responds negatively, thus fueling even more annoying behavior.

Instead, what you want to do is begin to use some reverse psychology. Make him/her feel like your new best friend! Disguise any hint of negativity when you respond to this student. Start, simply, by saying three nice things to this student today. Here are just a few examples: "How's your day going today? I hope it's great!" "I love your shirt. Is that new?" "Thanks for getting busy on your work. I really appreciate that." "That was a really clever answer. I love your creativity!" "I like the way you helped your group today. I noticed that and I appreciate it." You get the point. Spread your compliments out. Don't give all three at one time. And know that you can say as many nice things as you'd like. You're not limited to three, but please commit to three at the very least.

Will three simple compliments remove any trace of annoying behavior from this particular student's personality? Hardly. But will it begin to change your relationship with this student, nudging it in a more positive direction? Absolutely. There are few things more powerful than a well-placed compliment.

Aggravating students become more aggravating when we act as though they are aggravating us. They feed off of the reactions of others. If you stop acting as though you are annoyed by their behavior and start noticing the things that are *not* annoying and complimenting those things instead, you'll start seeing less annoying behavior. It's free, it's fun, it takes no extra work, and it generates amazingly positive results!

15

Post a Simple Sign Telling Why You're a Teacher

What to Do

Make a sign that says, "I am a teacher because..." and then list the reasons.

How and Why to Do It

Making this sign will take about five minutes. Make it fairly large (poster-board size or larger) so that it can be read from anywhere in the room. Write the title in big, bold letters. Here's an example:

I Am a Teacher Because. . .

1. I love my students.
2. I love to help people achieve their goals.

3. I believe that all of my students are talented. It is a privilege to help students discover their unique talents.
4. I believe that all of my students have amazing potential. It is a privilege to help all students realize their potential.
5. I feel there is no more important profession in the world.
6. I love learning from my students.
7. Teaching is fun for me!

Remember that your sign doesn't have to be fancy and it doesn't have to look pretty. The students won't notice anything but what the sign actually *says*. Post it in a place where all students will see it every day—preferably on the front wall of the classroom. You may also want to place a duplicate sign right outside your classroom door—so that *all* can see it. Students who walk past your room will read it. The students you don't teach will want to be in your classroom. Instant recruitment! Adults who walk past your room will read it. It will remind you, every day, of why you are here and why you do what you do. And, as an added bonus, administrators love teachers who proudly proclaim their love of teaching and post it for all to see.

16

Have Students Create a Student Wall

What to Do

Designate one wall of your classroom as The Student Wall. This wall is *for* the students, *about* the students, and created *by* the students.

How and Why to Do It

Teachers spend time, effort, and money decorating their classrooms, just as most people spend time, effort, and money decorating their homes. In many homes, refrigerators bear evidence of children's drawings, activity schedules, photos, etc. Walls throughout the house are adorned with photos and artwork. And children's rooms scream of their personalities. It would be rare to walk into a child's bedroom and not find numerous pictures of that child. All of these adornments make a house feel like a home.

For that very reason, it's important to make your classroom feel like a "home" for your students. And you don't have to spend money doing it. Let the students select the following:

1. A sample or two of pieces of schoolwork they are proud of.
2. A "selfie" they have taken.
3. Something like a piece of artwork, a picture of them receiving an award, a picture of them playing their favorite sport or engaging in a favorite activity, or even a picture of their pet animal!
4. Possibly a sentence or two to accompany their photo–saying who they are, what interests them, etc.

Now allow them to post these on The Student Wall. You, too, may want to write something you like about each student and post it next to each one's picture (see Tip 64). Take pictures of students while they are working in class and post a few of those on the student wall. And notice how much time they spend looking at the wall, beaming with pride.

This simple "student wall" will help them take ownership of the classroom. It will make the classroom feel like a second home to them. Your classroom will be one they *want* to come to–one where they feel safe, valued, and important!

17

Designate One Hour a Day for Paperwork

What to Do

Pick one hour of the day—be it early morning, immediately after school, or at night—that you can designate for uninterrupted planning and/or grading time. The key word is "uninterrupted." We'll explain below.

How and Why to Do It

How many hours a day does a typical teacher spend planning? That all depends, but many teachers will tell you they literally spend hours, every day, preparing lessons and grading papers. Upon further scrutiny, we continue to find that very few teachers have a specific time designated as planning/grading time. They do their paperwork sporadically—15 minutes before school begins, 20 minutes on a break, 10 minutes here and there once they get home (depending on the level of chaos at home), and any few minutes they can steal from their hectic days and nights. Can you relate? When asked, most teachers will admit that their phones and other electronic devices are always within reach. While doing paperwork, they answer phone calls, occasionally glance at social media posts, listen to daily news in the background, referee arguments between their children at home, do household chores, and you name it. And they never feel like they get caught up on their work... There just aren't enough hours in the day. Or are there?

Consider the fact that in ONE hour of uninterrupted planning time, you can accomplish more than you could in four hours of "interrupted" time. If you designate one specific hour each day for planning/grading and ensure that you are away from people and away from distractions (no phones, social media, music, television, or any other type of distraction), you will be amazed at what you can accomplish.

We're not guaranteeing that you will get all of your work done every day. We are, however, suggesting that you'll get more accomplished in one uninterrupted hour than you will over the span of several hours replete with distractions. What do you have to lose by *not* trying this? Precious time with family, time for yourself, and *sleep*!

18

Give Stickers!

What to Do

Do you want a very inexpensive, practically fool-proof way to motivate students, reward students, improve your classroom climate, and show that you care? Give students stickers.

How and Why to Do It

Before you start wondering if stickers are for the "young kids," go to a college football game. What do the players have (and want more of) on their helmets? Stickers! What do many people proudly put on their vehicles? Bumper stickers! What do you think tattoos are? They're permanent "stickers." What does almost everyone include in a text message? Emojis—virtual stickers!

People of all ages love stickers. Yet, in schools, we often see them used more in the elementary grades than in middle and high. This is a missed opportunity, as stickers may just be the most underrated and inexpensive motivator in education today!

We encourage you to go to almost any store or to shop online and buy some stickers. If you really don't want to spend a penny in order to prove the benefits of this technique, then ask a couple of your colleagues if they have any spare stickers to give to you. Someone in your school will be more than happy to shower you with free stickers.

Begin putting these stickers on test papers, student work samples, or on the students themselves! If a student does a good job at something, say, "You've just earned a sticker!" and place it on the student's hand. Or you can simply hand the sticker to them. They may put it on themselves or put it on their clothing or put it on one of their books. They may simply put it away. That's fine. Whether they display it or not, they received your message loudly and clearly: "I noticed that you did something well, and I appreciate you." It's amazing to see what students will do for a sticker!

Students yearn to be noticed, loved, and appreciated. Stickers are a fun, easy, inexpensive way to show your recognition, love, and appreciation.

19

Speed Up the Slow Starters

What to Do

Do you have a student (or two or three) who lags and drags when you tell the class to get started on an assignment? Today, you'll be implementing a trick for helping those slow or reluctant starters to begin their assignments more quickly. It simply involves pretending to assume that they're not understanding the material—even if you know they are—and then offering your assistance.

How and Why to Do It

This student is in every classroom—the one who intentionally drags his feet when everyone else gets busy on an assignment. (Note that we are not referring to a student who doesn't get busy because he doesn't understand how to do the work. That's a whole different issue.) You tell the student to get started. He pretends to get busy for a second but never quite manages to get there. You tell him yet again that he needs to start working.

He acts as though you're bothering him. You inevitably become upset, and he knows it. The power struggle has begun. After much cajoling and possibly threatening on your part, he reluctantly starts working. But he's already far behind the others. The struggle is real in many classrooms.

Try this instead: The next time it happens that the student is stalling, don't get mad. Or at least don't *act* mad. Pretend to assume that you know he wants to do the work and the fact that he isn't working must mean he doesn't understand. Go to him and whisper,

> I notice you're having trouble getting started. Do you not understand? How can I help? I'll tell you what—we'll get started together. And remember that any time you're having trouble, I'm only a few feet away. My job is to help you, and I'm happy to do that.

Display a calm, kind demeanor. And help him to get busy. The key is to avoid any semblance of a power struggle.

If the student thinks you're upset and that he's controlling your emotions, he'll keep exhibiting the same, if not worse, behavior. Once he thinks you are on his side and realizes that you will help him to get busy when he's not, there's simply no reason not to do his work. Try it!

20

Make Participation Less Stressful

What to Do

Today, you'll be using a technique that takes the pressure off of students when they are asked to answer questions in front of their peers. You'll do this by simply pairing students, allowing them to think through their answers together.

How and Why to Do It

Getting students to actively participate can sometimes be a daunting task. You teach something, and then you begin to ask a few questions. Who raises their hands? Often, the same two or three students. Some students, whom you know have the correct answer, will not even make eye contact with you, much less raise their hands to volunteer an answer. Are they lazy? Do they simply not care? Are they trying to rebel by not participating? Unlikely. What's highly likely, however, is that many students don't want to risk having a wrong answer or simply don't want to risk any type of embarrassment in front of their peers. But we have a way around that.

Put your students in pairs. Begin your discussion, ask a question, and say, "Don't tell me. Tell your partner. I'll give you two minutes to discuss with your partner what you think the answer may be. Go!" And voila! Everyone is participating. While they are discussing, walk around and listen, offering assistance if necessary. You can learn a whole lot by listening in on student discussions.

When the two minutes are up, start pointing to pairs of students and say, "What did you two come up with?" Notice how willing they are now to share their answers. You've removed the intimidation factor. You're asking them to think deeply and bounce their thoughts off of a fellow student. Some students, while discussing with another, will begin to think differently about the answer. Some may correct an incorrect answer.

When asked why this technique makes participating in class discussions easier, a student summed it up beautifully: "It's easier to look stupid with someone else as opposed to by myself. If we get the answer wrong together, it's not so embarrassing." Ah, from the mouths of babes...

21

Defuse a Negative Coworker

What to Do

Have you ever noticed how negative coworkers can put a damper on your positive mood? Heck, they can suck the life out of you! Not anymore. We'll show you how to defuse a negative coworker with a few simple words, all while maintaining your enthusiastic, positive image and your precious peace of mind.

Instead of getting pulled down by their negativity, on your next encounter, simply begin asking questions or making simple statements that will leave them scratching their heads and looking for another target on which to spew their bitterness. Here's how.

How and Why to Do It

Here she comes, Nagatha Nelson, the self-appointed nay-sayer of the school. You don't have to be psychic to know that she will latch onto anyone who will listen to her. She will bad-mouth either the administrators, the students, the parents, or teaching in general. She has no other topics of discussion. Her sour attitude can poison anyone within earshot or eyeshot.

You try to steer clear of her, but she's unavoidable because she seems to show up everywhere. What can you do? The next time she says something negative, say, "Are you feeling okay? You don't seem like yourself today. May I help?" And watch for her reaction. Shock factor can be a beautiful thing.

If she speaks negatively of a student, simply say, "Oh, I love that kid." Even if you don't know that student, pretend you do. Then smile, tell her you have to rush off because you have a deadline to meet, and walk away. Each time you encounter her, use the same approach. Just ask a simple question or make a simple, positive statement. Soon, she'll be avoiding *you* just the way you used to avoid *her*!

It's time that we stop giving negative people a stage and an audience. They won't perform if the audience doesn't show up. If enough coworkers realize this, you can turn out the lights, close the curtains, and lock the door to that theater once and for all.

22

Befriend a New Teacher

What to Do

Find the newest, most inexperienced teacher in the school, and befriend her. Introduce yourself. Tell her you're happy that she's joined the faculty. And offer to help if she has questions.

How and Why to Do It

Know, in advance, that many people will be trying to become the new kid on the block's "new best friend." We're not suggesting you compete to become her new best friend. We are simply suggesting that you offer your assistance to this new teacher, within reason, of course. It takes only a little time (and makes a *big* difference) to ask how she is doing, to answer simple questions she may have, and to serve as a positive role model. Yes, the negative teachers tend to attach themselves quickly to the new teachers in an attempt to "recruit them." You can't control that. But you can become a trusted, helpful friend to those who need it most. Also, tell the new teacher that you look forward to learning from her as well, as new teachers bring loads of fresh ideas.

If you encounter the new teacher in the hallway, ask how things are going. If she needs ideas, share yours. If she's struggling with something, either offer to help or direct her to someone who can. Invite her into your classroom to see you in action. Allowing a new teacher to observe you takes no extra time at all, as you're teaching anyway. And new teachers are like sponges—they'll gratefully absorb any helpful hints you can share.

We all remember what it was like to be new and inexperienced, afraid to ask questions for fear of appearing incompetent. And we can all remember the people who helped us through that trying first year. Be that person for a new teacher. An added bonus is that by helping others, we help ourselves. Be open to learning from their fresh ideas, their struggles, and their accomplishments.

23

Become Better Organized in 10 Minutes!

What to Do

Today, we'll show you how to spend a mere 10 minutes—
no more than that—becoming better organized. Even if
you're already well-organized, you can always be even
better organized. You'll do this by (1) throwing a few
items out, and (2) putting a reminder pad on your desk.
You may actually be able to do this in less than 10 minutes.

How and Why to Do It

Everyone *wants* to become better organized—so much so
that there are businesses that offer organizational services,
shows on television where willing participants allow professional organizers to make over their spaces, and stores
that sell nothing but containers for organization. But many
people continue to struggle through life amid chaos and
disorganization. Some of these people are teachers. If you

can relate, we have an easy way to help you begin conquering your chaos.

Take two simple steps today: (1) Either throw out or donate 10 items in your classroom that you don't need or don't use, and (2) Put a reminder pad on your desk so that you have quick access to it at all times. Don't trust your memory. Write what you need to do that day on the reminder pad. If you have an app for this purpose, use the physical notepad anyway. It's so much quicker to jot a reminder on the pad as opposed to getting your phone, unlocking it, opening your app, and typing your item into the list. If you want to add the information to your app later, that's fine.

Now imagine taking one step each day toward better organization. Maybe tomorrow you'll organize one drawer of your desk. Maybe the next day you'll file the folders that have been sitting on that shelf. Maybe the day after that you'll organize the second drawer of your desk. You get the point. Baby steps, one day at a time.

You may never be perfectly organized, but each day you can become a little better organized. Just set aside a few minutes and eat away at your clutter one bite at a time. We'll show you how to get some free help in the next tip.

There's no question that organized classrooms run more efficiently, and organized teachers are more effective and productive—because they know where their stuff is!

24

Get a Free Classroom Makeover

What to Do

Could your classroom use a little sprucing up, straightening out, or rearranging? If so, there's a way to get a classroom makeover without spending any money—and, possibly, without doing any work! You'll only need to find someone who loves to decorate and organize, and then turn that person loose on your classroom. We'll show you how.

How and Why to Do It

Have you ever had a room in your home redecorated, rearranged, or even cleaned and organized? Immediately following, you didn't want to leave that room. You just wanted to look at it and enjoy it. It felt good to be in that room—somehow peaceful, calm, and inviting. And that's exactly how we want students to feel every day in our classrooms. We all spend a lot of time there, so why not make it feel like home?

It's a well-known fact that talented, creative, interior-design-loving people are on every campus. Their classrooms are beautiful. Find these people and ask for their help in your own classroom. They *love* to do this! Tell them you have no money to spend. They love that type of challenge even more! They can use what you already have, donate items to you that they don't need, make suggestions for de-cluttering and organizing, ask you to bring simple items from home that you don't use, etc. They make simple changes like rearranging the furniture, painting an old shelf, creating a small space for students to relax, listen to music, read a book, etc. They work wonders with donated crates for storing, organizing, and decluttering. Give them a few hours to work their magic, and you won't recognize your classroom. Then praise them profusely and tell *everyone* about them. Put a sign in your room that says, "Decorated by _____." If you can't find a teacher, there is probably a talented parent who would love to have a crack at decorating your classroom. Just ask.

We know a teacher who got a local interior designer to donate his time. Using items the teacher already had and items her fellow teachers were happy to get rid of, he spent an afternoon redecorating her room. In return, the school thanked him in its newsletter and also on the marquee out front.

Results? Your classroom now looks amazing. It is better organized, more comfortable, and more appealing to the students. And you are now able to run the classroom more effectively and efficiently. All of this with a zero budget and free labor!

25

Try the "Have You Noticed" Trick

What to Do

This trick is designed to change student behavior. By using it, you'll be helping students with undesirable behaviors to behave in a more desirable manner. It involves catching the students when they're *not* exhibiting negative behaviors and asking if they have noticed that they've been acting more appropriately lately. We'll explain below.

How and Why to Do It

This trick is so simple. Let's say that Lizzie is a chronic talker. You've been speaking to her about it, punishing her when the behavior gets out of hand, and basically begging her to just *stop talking*! Most of this to no avail... So now it's time to try a simple trick that employs the use of good old reverse psychology. You wait for an opportunity when Lizzie is not talking, and you immediately go to her (out of earshot of her classmates) and say,

> Lizzie, have you noticed that you're not talking out of turn as much? That shows a great deal of restraint and maturity on your part. I wanted you to know that I've noticed it also, and I'm proud of you. Do you mind if I write your mom a note and tell her how proud I am?

And then you write the note telling her mom that you're proud of the fact that Lizzie is not talking out of turn as much. (The beauty in this note is that you are actually letting her mom know that there *is* a problem. However, you're doing it in a positive manner, saying how proud you are that she's doing a little better.) Then continue to catch Lizzie behaving appropriately.

Regardless of their age, students love being complimented. And the older they get, the rarer it is that their parents and/or guardians receive compliments about them. So, by using this trick, you're helping to reverse that trend. The students and their parents feel more positive about you, and, most importantly, the students feel more positive about themselves.

So you're "tricking" students into behaving? You're using manipulative tactics on students? Absolutely. We're teachers. We'll try any trick in the book if it meets the following requirements: It's safe, it's free, it helps students to behave and perform better, and it makes classroom life more pleasant. Score!

26

Shift Your Focus

What to Do

Instead of asking yourself, "What am I going to teach today?" ask "What are my students going to learn today?" Sounds pretty simple, right? It is, and it can make a profound difference in your effectiveness.

How and Why to Do It

At first glance, asking "What are my students going to learn?" as opposed to "What am I going to teach?" may appear to be just a matter of semantics, but it's not. What you're doing is shifting your focus away from what *you* will do and placing it squarely on what the *students* will accomplish. We often suggest that teachers begin almost every sentence of their lesson plans with "The students will..." By doing this, you can dramatically improve the way you plan your lessons.

We'll give you the simplest scenario possible. Let's say that you are planning to begin a lesson today by introducing a concept as simple as addition. When planning your lesson, you may write that you'll define and explain the concept of addition to the students. Notice that that is stated in terms of what *you* will do, and it seems to assume that the students will be sitting passively and hopefully listening as you explain. But if you shift your focus to what the *students* will do, you may just change the activity to something like this: The students will manipulate jelly beans while the teacher introduces the concept of addition. Everyone will start with one jelly bean placed in a circle on their paper. The teacher will ask them to "add" one jelly bean to the circle. Then the students will determine how many jelly beans are now in the circle. The teacher will then say, "That's it. Now you understand addition!" And the lesson will progress from there.

Which of those two activities do you think the students would prefer? Listening passively or participating actively? Though this was a very simple example, the technique will work in any subject at any grade level. A change in thinking forces a change in action.

When you shift your focus from what the teacher will do to what the learners will do, you improve the way you plan and thus the way you teach!

27

Convince Your Students. . .

What to Do

With the right attitude and approach, you can convince your students of practically anything. Use this to your benefit in order to convince your students that you are always happy to see them when they arrive each day and always sad when they leave you. We'll show you how.

How and Why to Do It

Remember that students who believe you genuinely care about them will stop at nothing to please you. Putting forth a little effort to convince students that you truly care about them will reward you a hundredfold. Students have to be convinced that you love teaching and you love them!

Now let's be realistic—are you always elated to see every student every day? Of course not. Are there days when you are possibly even relieved that a particular student is absent? If so, know that you're not alone. It's normal to feel this way on some days. But the students can never know that you feel this way. If you want to get the most from your students and for them to get the most from you, then you have to convince them of two things: You're elated to see them when they arrive, and you miss them when they leave. Tell them this! And let them know that weekends are a little sad for you, because you miss them. Summer break is almost painful! Yeah, right.

Effective teachers always work at convincing students of the two things we just mentioned—appearing happy when students arrive and just a little sad when they leave. How do they do it? It's easy: First, you *tell* the students how, basically, your life revolves around them. You can't wait to see them each day and you're downright sad when they leave. Before holiday breaks, remind them of how much you will miss them. On Friday afternoons, remind them that you can't wait for Monday morning. And at the end of the year, squeeze out a few tears if you can! But don't stop telling them how much they mean to you and how lucky you feel to be teaching them. If you doubt the effectiveness of this simple act, you've obviously never tried it. Try it now. You've got nothing to lose and your students have everything to gain.

28

Know the Simple Dos and Don'ts of Social Media*

What to Do

Don't be afraid to *use* social media. Just be sure never to *abuse* social media.

How and Why to Do It

Social media platforms present countless possibilities for connecting with students, parents, friends, family, and colleagues. Just be clear about what's appropriate and what's not. Here are a few of the general *dos* and *don'ts* regarding the use of social media:

Do:

♦ Adhere to your school's and/or district's social media policy.

◆ Use social media to set up class pages, connect with parents, post assignments, and do anything within your school's guidelines that helps promote student success.

◆ Connect with other educators, worldwide, via social media (we show you how in Tip 29).

◆ Remember that even if your account is private, you never know who may share your posts or, worse yet, hack into them.

Don't:

◆ Post anything online that you wouldn't want your students, their parents, or your administrators to see.

◆ Use personal social media sites during work hours.

◆ Complain about work, students, parents, or coworkers on social media sites.

Remember that maintaining a positive reputation is essential to earning the trust of students, parents, colleagues, administrators, and the community. If you're ever in doubt as to whether something is appropriate or not, don't post it. Always err on the side of caution, because once it's out there in cyberspace, you can't take it back!

* Adapted from Breaux and Whitaker, *Seven Simple Secrets*, pp 88, 89.

29

Get Free Ideas via Twitter

What to Do

Twitter may just be the best-kept secret for educators. If you're not already on Twitter, take five minutes to sign up. You'll soon be in touch with some of the most dynamic, innovative, positive educators on Earth. If you're not into "tweeting," that's fine. You can still get free ideas from other knowledgeable educators without anyone even knowing you're there. Lurk and learn!

How and Why to Do It

When we use social media and its resources with the goal of improving professionally, it allows the knowledge of one to become the knowledge of many. It's reassuring to connect with other educators who share a similar philosophy. And it's so easy to find new ideas that you can implement in your own classroom instantly. Whether it's as simple as getting bulletin board ideas or lesson plan ideas or as complex as integrating current events into a cross-curricular unit that ties in with state standards, the answers are out there in the Twitterverse. Do a search relating to current challenges you are facing, and you'll usually find that someone has already solved the same problem and has shared their answers on Twitter.

As stated earlier, you can simply lurk and learn or join any of the countless educational chats that take place daily. There are chats for first-grade teachers and chats for physics teachers. Chats for general education and special education. Chats for new teachers and chats for veteran teachers. Chats for increasing parental involvement. Chats for improving classroom management. You name it, and there's a chat for it.

For a list of current chats, go to https://sites.google.com/site/twittereducationchats/education-chat-calendar.

Not only can Twitter provide specific lesson plan ideas, content, and concepts, but it can also provide a much-needed emotional boost. You, too, can help others by sharing your own ideas if you choose.

Could you use a little inspiration, camaraderie, or free ideas for improving your teaching? You're sure to find it when you connect with others on Twitter.

30

Compliment the Custodian

What to Do

Today, we'd like you to make a simple gesture—
compliment at least one of the custodians. Better yet,
compliment all of them! We'll show you how and explain
why this is so important.

How and Why to Do It

For a school to function effectively, it takes the entire team—
the administrative assistants, the food service workers, the
school nurses, the teaching assistants, the bus drivers, the
teachers, the administrators, and, probably most importantly, the custodians! They have the ability to make your
life either miserable or joyous, don't they? They are unsung
heroes who usually escape the limelight, but none of us can
deny that what they do is vital to the way our school and
classrooms function. What a custodian does or doesn't do
can impact our ability to focus on teaching and learning
every day. Your school may have a team of maintenance

workers or possibly just one or two, but each of them deserves our recognition, admiration, and appreciation. When we treat people with respect, they perform better. It's that simple.

So how can you show your appreciation to one (or all) of the custodians? You can do something as simple as leaving a sticky note on your trash can thanking them for all they do. You can thank them in person. Leave an occasional candy bar with a thank-you note from you and your students. Not that you are doing it for this reason, but believe us when we say you will now receive preferential treatment from the custodial staff. They'll go out of their way to clean a spill, move a bookcase, find an extra table or desk for you, etc.

But what if the custodian who cleans your classroom is not exactly performing at peak levels? Then it's even more important to show your appreciation. Chances are good that they will now put forth extra effort, at least in your classroom.

Can something as simple as complimenting a custodian make you a better teacher? Yes, it can. By making others feel special, it makes *you* feel good. And when you involve the students in showing appreciation to others, it makes them feel good. Your room likely gets more custodial attention than it used to because showing appreciation and respect becomes a reciprocal action. When we all feel good, we all perform better. Everyone wins!

31

Ask for Student Feedback on Your Teaching

What to Do

Take a few minutes to find out what your students think about your teaching. Note that this is different from what you did in Tip 7 where you asked for feedback on a particular lesson. This time, you're asking for feedback on your teaching in general. Be prepared for some good, honest feedback. And try not to be afraid of what they may say. Who better to tell you how you're doing than your students?

How and Why to Do It

Tell the students you'd like to know how they feel about your teaching and about the way you treat each of them. Also, tell them that you'll be asking them to give you their feedback anonymously (in a questionnaire) because you want their honest opinions, even if negative. You'll have a student collect all of these at the end of class and leave them on your desk. Stress that your goal is to find out how well they feel you are or are not doing your job because you are always striving to improve in any way possible. Tell them you'll read each of their answers and suggestions carefully and though you may not be able to implement all suggestions, you'll certainly use their feedback to help you to be the best teacher you can be.

Keep it simple. Do this once or, better yet, do it every quarter! Here's a sample of the types of questions to ask:

1. Do you feel that I do my best to help you to do your best?
2. Do you feel that I treat you fairly and respectfully?
3. Do you feel that you are important to me and that I care about you?
4. Do you have any suggestions for me regarding how I might improve my teaching?

What do you accomplish by doing this? You receive honest feedback and suggestions for improvement. Will all suggestions be doable? Probably not. But some will be. Also, you send the message to your students that their opinions matter, that you're striving to be better, and that you're open to accepting constructive criticism. That's what positive role models do; that's how successful businesses are operated; that's how we would like to be treated by anyone providing a service to us; and that's what students in every classroom deserve!

32

Sell What You're Teaching!

What to Do

The easiest way to "sell" what you're teaching is to act as though what you're teaching is important and relevant. Sure, anything we teach should be important and relevant, but the students won't know that unless we *act* as though it is.

How and Why to Do It

If the title of this book had been "Information for Teachers," you may have never picked it up. Even if the book was given to you, you may have never bothered to open it. The title had to convince you that this book is filled with techniques that can improve your teaching—in an *easy* way and with *instant* results. We already knew the book was important and relevant, but you didn't. So, we put a lot of thought into *how* to get you to see that the information contained within is worthwhile, helpful, and not overwhelming. We didn't share *easy* techniques because we think you're lazy. We shared *easy* techniques because we wanted to make each one doable!

Now, we'd like for you to use that same concept with your students. Make your lessons doable, fun, interesting, and exciting. If a concept is overwhelming, many of the students will simply give up. If the students don't think they will ever use this skill in their lives, they won't put much effort into learning it.

Have you ever heard a student say, "I'm no good at math"? That's a student who has never been taught that math is everywhere. Without it, there are no phones, no tablets, no televisions, no houses, no restaurants, no grocery stores, and no "anything." If you throw a football, you use math. The football was made using math. But many students think math happens in books and on boring worksheets and that it has no relevance in their lives—because we forgot to "sell" it to them.

The way you approach each lesson involves the same concept as determining the best title (and content) for a book. You're the *cover* and you're the *content*. Sell your book to your students by acting as though what you're teaching is important. Say, "I can hardly wait to show you what we'll be learning today!" Spend some time convincing them that each skill will be doable and that they will be able to actually *use* it in their lives. And then walk them through whatever skill you are teaching—making it relevant, understandable, and doable. The key is that you have to act enthusiastically throughout the lesson. (We'll show you how to do that in Tip 35.)

33

Let Students Run a Project from Start to Finish

What to Do

This tip will take the workload off of *you* and place the responsibility on the *students*. They'll be completing a project from start to finish. You'll simply be guiding them, but they'll be doing most of the work. Of course, you'll be adapting this to accommodate your particular grade level. Very young students will need a little more guidance. Okay, a lot more...

How and Why to Do It

We stole this particular idea from a fifth-grade teacher, but it can be used in any grade you choose and modified to fit the age level and/or subject matter: Students work in pairs and do research on a particular historical figure. Each pair is assigned a different person. This project can lend itself to famous mathematicians, scientists, authors, inventors, etc. The idea is to present each pair of students with some specific project guidelines and then set them free. Once their research is complete, one student (in each pair) will be the interviewer and one will act as the famous figure. On a designated day, they each "dress the part." No, they don't need fancy costumes. One dresses the way a journalist would dress and the other wears something representative of the famous figure (as simple as a construction paper hat, mustache, etc.).

Each interviewer asks the same questions which have been pre-determined by you. Example: What is your name? Where and when were you born? What was your childhood like? What was your greatest achievement? What was your greatest failure? These interviews are recorded on video, either by you or by a student. Then, a student (or you, if you don't want to give up total control—ha!) takes all videos and combines them into one. The class watches the video together and learns about lots of historical figures. All students receive a grade for their video. Finally, a copy is sent home for them to keep and share with family members.

Student pride in such a project is palpable. And they do almost all of the work. You are simply a *guide on the side.* You can use this idea and apply it to almost any type of project in any subject area. The students love it, the parents love it, everyone learns, and everyone wins!

34

Use One Piece of Test Data to Improve Your Effectiveness

What to Do

Test data—two words that tend to evoke negative reactions from teachers and students. We realize how overwhelming test data can be. But remember, we're trying to help you have *less* stress, not more. Therefore, we're going to show you how to start with only one piece of test data to literally change the way you are teaching. We're only asking that you try it once, for now.

How and Why to Do It

So much data. So little time. It can swallow us whole, can't it? There's no way to do it all, so you may be tempted to bury your head in the sand and do nothing. Instead, merely use one piece of data to improve your teaching.

Whether it's data from state-wide tests or a classroom test doesn't really matter. All tests provide results, and how we *use* the results can help or hinder student progress. Let's use a simple classroom test as an example. Suppose that you gave a test on *identifying the main idea* in a piece of writing. The test results revealed that most of your students did not thoroughly understand the skill. So, take that one piece of data and use it to re-teach the skill differently because it's obvious that the first way you taught it did not yield positive results. While re-teaching any skill, ensure that the students are engaged. Practice the skill with them before you send them off to try it on their own. Once you feel confident that they understand more thoroughly, test again. Results are guaranteed to be better this time because understanding is better.

Will everyone understand all concepts perfectly? Of course not. But taking one small step in using data to drive your instruction is better than taking no steps. We hope you will continue this practice and begin using assessment data to drive your instruction, but even if you only do it once, you're now more effective than you were before you did it. Improved instruction leads to higher student achievement. It seems so over-simplified, but this is what using test data means—finding out what students don't understand and teaching them in a way that will help them to understand it better. You may not ever do it all, but you can take one step, no matter how small.

35

Act More Enthusiastic Than You Feel

What to Do

We're asking you to try something, just for a day. We're convinced that when you see the results, it will become a daily habit from here forward. For one day, act more enthusiastic than you feel and pretend to be happier than you are. That's it, plainly and simply.

How and Why to Do It

In Tip 32, we addressed the fact that you have to "sell" what you're teaching. Whether you feel your best today or not, the students still need and deserve a positive teacher who loves *teaching*, loves the *content*, and loves *them*. Effective teachers remind themselves daily that they are actors on a stage. They are constantly working at acting happier and more enthusiastic than they feel, even if they are already feeling happy and enthusiastic. On days when they don't feel even a twinge of happiness or enthusiasm, they fake it.

Try this simple tactic: Pretend that you won the lottery, and act, all day, like you would act if you knew you now had a gazillion dollars and didn't ever *have* to work again. Don't tell the students what you're doing or why. Just *act* extremely happy and enthusiastic. Within seconds, you will see a difference in the attitudes and actions of the students.

Here are a few student reactions you can expect to see: Some will ask if you are okay, some will look at one another as if to ask, "What's going on?" and many will unknowingly "catch" your enthusiasm. Just observe and enjoy. Notice everything about their reactions, and notice how they interact with you, with each other, and with class activities today. Initially, you will likely witness confusion, bewilderment, and skepticism (Is she really that happy?). This will quickly give way to buy-in (Okay, she's really happy today. We don't know why, but she is.). Finally, you'll see your own enthusiasm becoming theirs.

Who doesn't win big in this scenario? And you can do this every single day. Why wouldn't you? It's free, it's fun, and it works! Try it just for a day, however, and allow the students to convince you that how *you* act has a significant impact on how *they* act!

36

Delegate Classroom Duties

What to Do

Make a brief list of tasks that need to be done around the room each day—tasks that can be done by *students* as opposed to those that require an adult to accomplish. Then start delegating responsibility to your students. Stop doing all of the work and help them to become more responsible.

How and Why to Do It

Let's look at some examples of items you may have on your list: Collecting an assignment, passing out an assignment, sharpening pencils, straightening desks or tables, handing out supplies for a project or activity, picking up trash around the room, changing the day's date, turning a projector on and off, welcoming a visitor, or anything else you can imagine. These tasks can be as simple as closing the door when class begins and opening it when the class leaves. If school policy dictates that you must be the one to close and lock the door, then give one student the task of reminding you to do that.

You may want to share the list with your students and have them "sign up" for a job this week. Or you may want to assign certain jobs to particular students for specific reasons. Some jobs involve everyone's participation. For example, all are responsible for picking up any trash around their desks. About 30 seconds before the dismissal bell, have them "clean the room." The custodians will love you for it!

Other jobs require certain types of students. For instance, if one of the jobs on your list is "gofer," one who may occasionally deliver something to a teacher down the hall or the main office, you won't want that job assigned to a student who can't even be trusted when you're watching. Use your good judgment, of course. And allow students to change jobs from time to time.

Students of all ages actually enjoy having assigned jobs. Delegating certain responsibilities to students helps them to take ownership of, and pride in, the classroom. It makes them feel important. When everyone plays a role, the classroom can run like a well-oiled machine.

37

Observe Other Teachers

What to Do

In every school there are teachers doing amazing, innovative things. We hear students, parents, and other educators singing their praises. On some occasions these colleagues are recognized by receiving awards or other types of special acclamation. So, it's only natural that we're curious about what these teachers are doing. Sometimes we may even be a bit envious. There's actually a simple way to find out what they're doing: Go into their classrooms and observe them. Then simply incorporate what they're doing into your own practice.

How and Why to Do It

One of the scariest things about teaching is that we're never quite sure of how good we are or are not. Are we using the best techniques? Are our students really understanding thoroughly? Are there more effective and efficient ways to accomplish our goals? Sadly, we seldom see our peers actually teaching in their classrooms. Yet, when we observe others, we can gather (teachers call it stealing!) new ideas much more quickly than by just reading articles or attending professional development seminars. At a professional development seminar, you may learn a lot about something like Project-Based Learning. But you'll learn even more about Project-Based Learning if you can see it in action, in a classroom, in your own school! It goes without saying that the better the teacher you observe, the better the ideas you can steal.

Set up a time (and acquire permission) to go and observe an excellent teacher. You don't need an hour. You can learn a lot in just a few minutes when you observe an effective teacher in action. The good news is that the best teachers are more than willing to share ideas and allow others to come in and observe them. Don't be surprised if they ask to come and steal ideas from you. New teachers, too, tend to have an array of knowledge regarding the newest techniques, so you may want to observe them, also. When you observe others, you get great ideas for room arrangement, management techniques, teaching strategies, bulletin boards, ways to use technology, etc.

By seeing our colleagues teach—and inviting them into our rooms—we all start to implement best practices. It all starts with one observation, but it never stops there. Start by observing the best, of course. Going forward, observe all who will open their doors to you, and steal away!

38

Simplify Your Management Plan

What to Do

The foundation of any effective teacher's classroom is the classroom management plan—a plan created by the teacher, implemented consistently, and known to all. At its core are a few clear rules and lots of procedures. The best plans are the simplest ones, so we'd like to show you how to simplify yours.

How and Why to Do It

Without exception, all great teachers are great classroom managers. And all of their plans are similar in scope and simple in nature. Students know what is expected of them because the plan has been discussed and practiced, and it's implemented consistently. If students forget, or do not comply with, any aspect of the plan, they are simply reminded or re-taught when necessary.

The most critical components of any management plan are simplicity, clarity, and consistency. But many teachers get caught in the weeds. Their plans are unclear, lengthy, and inconsistent, often changing with the teacher's mood. Just in case there are a few weeds in your classroom management garden, there's a way to get it back into shape. Here's a checklist for simplifying your management plan:

- ◆ *Have I kept my rules to a minimum?* You'll want no more than five rules, reserved for serious offenses. If a rule is broken, there's a logical consequence.
- ◆ *Have I established clear procedures (ways of doing things), and do my students know what is expected of them?* You'll have lots of procedures for things such as how to enter and exit the room, how to turn in papers, what to do if you need a bathroom break, how to treat others, what to do if you have a question, how to get into and out of groups, what to do during emergencies, etc.
- ◆ *Am I consistent in implementing my management plan?*

Students respond well to structure because it works! But it's up to us to provide that structure. They deserve to know what is expected of them. But remember, they're students, and they'll need lots of ongoing reminders, practice, and guidance. Remember these three words: Simplicity, clarity, and consistency!

39

Shorten Classroom Activities

What to Do

Most teachers will agree that it's difficult to get students to focus on any one task for more than a few minutes at a time, *if* that long. Yet we need their focus the entire class period, don't we? If you want to maintain student focus for *longer*, you have to make your activities *shorter*.

How and Why to Do It

Did you ever give students an assignment that was going to take them more than 10 minutes to complete? If you did, did you notice that some got busy immediately and others didn't? That some finished early? That others also finished early but didn't do the assignment correctly? That some lagged so far behind that there was no finish line in sight? Did you hear the side conversations? Did you notice how hard you had to work to get them to refocus?

How is it that these same students can focus on their video games for hours? It's because of the segmented nature of video games. You start small and practice at one level. Then you advance to the next. How is it that some of your students who can't focus five minutes in class can focus on the field while playing an entire football game? Because the game is broken into many short segments called "plays." Likewise, break your activities into shorter segments. If they have to read a story, break that story up. Get them excited to begin reading it with some teasers. Do a short activity where they will predict what the story may be about based solely on the title. Then, have them read only the opening paragraph to see if anyone predicted correctly. Now, give them one or two things to look for in the next paragraph. You get the point. If it's a math problem, break it into steps—small, doable segments that go from simple to more complex. When your lessons consist of small segments, no single activity is long and boring.

The shorter the activity, the longer you can hold their attention. Also, the shorter the activity, the less chance there is that some students will finish far ahead of the others.

You've probably noticed that this book is written in small, attainable segments for the very same reason; great teachers maintain better student focus by teaching in small, attainable segments. Make your activities *shorter*, and you'll hold their attention *longer*!

40

Hold Classroom Raffles

What to Do

We'll preface this one by stating that this has nothing to do with school fundraising. Rather, it has to do with "fun-raising" in your own classroom. How do you *raise the fun* in a quick, easy way? Hold a classroom raffle!

How and Why to Do It

Classroom raffles are simply fun raffles where drawings are held and students win prizes. The raffles can be spontaneous or planned. It's your call. And the raffle items don't have to cost money—well, maybe you'll buy a few stickers. But you can raffle things like five minutes of free time, a free homework pass, an opportunity to sit at the teacher's desk, etc. Use your imagination and raffle anything you think your students will like.

A teacher shared his system with us:

I have a simple ticket system and a raffle jar. Students can earn tickets for turning in homework or projects, behaving well in class, behaving well at an assembly, volunteering to help others, participating in class activities, and more. I even raffle chances for them to help wash the teachers' cars during teacher appreciation week. The students love it, even though it means more work for them! At other times, I auction off something as simple as a sticker. I get almost all of my raffle prizes from local businesses. To get these, all I have to do is ask. Businesses donate restaurant coupons, ice cream, candy, movie tickets, gift cards, school supplies, and lots of other cool prizes. I save the best items for planned raffles. For instance, if I want all students to turn in homework assignments over an extended period of time, I hold up a brand new (donated) pair of headphones and say, "This will be raffled in two weeks. Anyone who doesn't miss a homework assignment for the next two weeks will be included in the raffle." At other times, I stop in mid-stream while teaching and say, "I feel a raffle coming. Then I reach into my raffle jar, pull a ticket out, and give a random prize to a winning student." It takes less than 30 seconds, and my students love it. They'll do almost anything to earn tickets! It's a fun way to motivate them, keep them on their toes, and reward them.

Be a "fun-raiser"!!!

41

Invite Outsiders In

What to Do

Invite someone noteworthy, or possibly even someone famous, to pay your class a visit via an online chat, text, tweet, or other social platform.

How and Why to Do It

Though it would be fantastic if you could get someone famous or noteworthy to stop by in person, that's not always easy to accomplish. The idea is to try to bring an outside voice inside your classroom—someone who can offer words of encouragement or inspiration to your students.

Though we don't consider ourselves famous, we will be more than happy to participate in this activity. Simply send us a tweet (@AnnetteBreaux and @ToddWhitaker) and include the hashtag #75WaystoBeaBetterTeacherTomorrow, and we'll send a tweet of encouragement to you and your students. You might be surprised to learn how many people will be eager to participate. But it doesn't have to be someone famous. It can be a friend of yours who is a teacher in another school and can send a message to the class saying they heard the class was doing really well in _____ (whatever subject, lesson, or project you choose), and so they just wanted to wish them well and encourage them to keep up the hard work. And now the students know that "the word is out" that they are important! Try contacting a famous author, singer, actor, speaker, or anyone else whose voice you feel would inspire your students. The more positive voices you can bring to them, the better.

A teacher shared the following with us:

> I have a student whose father is in the military and has recently been deployed. We set up an online video chat with him. All of the students had the opportunity to interact with him and ask questions. He, in turn, offered wonderful words of encouragement to the class. He promised to stop by for an in-person visit when his tour of duty finishes.

Imagine the pride in this student's heart. His dad is now famous! And speaking of parents, teachers often invite parents into their classrooms to share particular skills or talents with the class. We encourage you to do this, also. But for this tip, we're simply suggesting that you find someone (and yes, it can most certainly be a parent) from the outside to offer words of encouragement or inspiration to your students. It's quick, it's simple, and it makes an impact!

42

Laugh with Your Students

What to Do

Have you heard any good jokes lately? If not, we'll tell you where to find some. Do you laugh with your students daily? If not, we'll show you how.

How and Why to Do It

Laughter has countless benefits for both our physical and emotional health. The old saying "Laughter is the best medicine" holds as true as ever. But isn't teaching serious business? Of course it is. But just because something is serious business—i.e. the education of our youth, our future—that does not mean it can't be fun and enjoyable.

But what if you don't have a stash of jokes and you aren't a natural comedian? No problem. You don't have to be. Do a quick online search for kid-friendly jokes. It only takes a minute to get lists of them. Also, tell funny (appropriate) stories of things that happen to you. Allow students to share jokes with the class, but approve them first.

Walk into your classroom tomorrow and say, "Knock, knock." [Who's there?] "Broken pencil." [Broken pencil who?] "Never mind. It's pointless." How easy is that? Who cares if it's corny? The students laugh. Some have to explain it to their classmates. Some act as though it isn't funny, but what they're actually conveying is this: "That's hilarious, but I'm way too cool to laugh." But it doesn't mean they don't appreciate your effort at bringing humor into the classroom.

We learn best when we *like* what we're learning, are having fun learning it, and are learning from a happy person. Remember that having a sense of humor does not mean you have to be funny. It just means you have to be fun. In many classrooms, the atmosphere is far too serious. The only laughter is coming from students who are misbehaving—and the teacher is getting mad and daring the laughter to continue. No, you can't be laughing all the time. But you can be laughing with your students daily. Plan to start interjecting some humor into your daily teaching activities.

Science tells us that laughter decreases stress, increases endorphins, and improves your immune system. Do you want to be calmer, happier, and healthier? Share a laugh!

43

Stop Trying to Be Perfect

What to Do

All we want for you to do today is to stop striving for perfection. If you're always striving for perfection, you're always feeling defeated! Feeling defeated leads to a mindset of self-doubt, self-loathing, and self-destruction. That's the *opposite* mindset of effective teachers. Therefore, stop it, please!

How and Why to Do It

Consider and accept the fact that *no one* has ever perfected the art of teaching. You will (and should) continue to learn to teach for the rest of your career and, hopefully, the rest of your life. There are no perfect teachers. But there are some who strive for perfection and are frazzled, frustrated, and quickly burning themselves out.

And then there are the highly-effective teachers—the great ones. These are the teachers who are aware of their imperfections, their personality quirks, their lack of knowledge in particular areas. They work daily toward improvement, not perfection. They make mistakes just like everyone else. They just try not to make the same mistakes twice. They appear happier and less stressed than the perfectionists. That's because they have set an attainable goal—improvement. The perfectionists are continually failing at being perfect. Thus, they're miserable.

So, should you just give in and say, "Hey, I'm not perfect," and continue to be exactly the way you are? Hopefully not. Strive to be better, but not perfect. If none of your students understand a concept and you finally get half of them to understand, that's improvement. But don't rest on your laurels and forget about the other half. Yes, we would love for all students to fully understand every concept we teach. But if you won't be happy until that happens, then you won't ever be happy.

This entire book has been designed to help you improve a little each day. And each suggestion finds its roots in the classrooms of effective teachers. Instant improvement on a daily basis, accomplished in small increments, leads to drastic changes in teacher effectiveness.

44

Don't Let Students Know When They Get to You

What to Do

Though we hope this becomes a habit, we're only asking that, just for today, you do not let the students know when they are pushing your buttons.

How and Why to Do It

Fact: We all have buttons. And there are certain students who have figured out how to push every one of those buttons. These students can tell—by our words and, particularly, by our body language—when they have gotten to us. They know how to make us turn beet red, they know how to make us change our breathing patterns, they know how to make us roll our eyes, and, sometimes, they know how to make us raise our voices, clench our teeth, and wish we had chosen another profession. When any of these things occur, the students have taken control, and they know it. Therefore, the misbehavior usually escalates.

But they're aggravating you, so what can you do? Though we never suggest that you don't hold students accountable for inappropriate behavior, we always suggest that you do so in a calm, professional manner. We're not asking you to *be* calm and composed. We're just asking you to *appear* calm and composed. (See Tip 68 for more on body language.)

Here's an example: Mark has an uncanny ability to push your buttons. During the lesson, he keeps blurting out ridiculous answers. He knows the correct answers, but he's trying to gain some attention and trying to control your emotions. Don't respond the way you usually do. Today, take him aside and ask if he is all right. Say something like, "I know how smart you are, but you seem confused today. Do you need for me to stay in with you at recess and re-teach that concept to you? I don't mind at all." We all know that Mark will not want to stay in at recess to be taught something he already knows. The key is to act as though you think he just doesn't understand. You don't act mad or frustrated. You simply notice that he is struggling and you offer to help him.

When students see that they can't frustrate you, they stop trying to frustrate you. It's not fun anymore if you aren't going to play the game.

Try this all day. Any time a student frustrates you, deal with the issue calmly. If you're struggling to accomplish this, resurrect that memory from Tip 35 about winning the lottery!

45

Call a Parent with Good News!

What to Do

Often, the simplest of gestures have the most profound results. And this is a simple one. Choose one student (just for today) and make a phone call to a parent or family member telling them about something positive the student has done. Be sure to smile the entire time you're speaking, because a smile can be heard over the phone!

How and Why to Do It

"Oh no, the teacher is calling!" Sadly, that's the way many families feel when they see the teacher's or school's number appear on his phone. That's because most phone calls between teachers and parents involve negative news. We can do something about this, however—maybe not every day, but definitely more often.

Select a student whose family often receives negative news regarding their performance or behavior in school. Now come up with a reason to bear good news: Maybe the student made a B on a math quiz, maybe you noticed when he was assisting another student in some way, maybe he turned in homework, or maybe the student just brought a pencil to class three days in a row! The student doesn't have to break a world record in order to earn a positive call to the family. If a student has two parents, you may want to think about which you'll call. If you call parents at work, chances are they may just broadcast the good news to the entire office!

Remember that every time you praise someone, at least two people feel better. One of those is you! In this case, at least three people feel better: You, the parent, and the student. That number grows exponentially as word begins to spread throughout the family. And now you've established a more positive relationship with the student's family. This will come in handy if you ever have to call with less-than-good news...

46

Become More "REAL" to Your Students

"...once you are Real you can't be ugly, except to people who don't understand."
— Margery Williams Bianco, *The Velveteen Rabbit*

What to Do

The more "real" we become in the eyes of our students, the better our chances of reaching and teaching them. Being "real" to someone is the foundation of a good relationship. Therefore, we'll show you how to take small, simple steps toward becoming more "real" to your students.

How and Why to Do It

Students are typically oblivious to the fact that their teachers have lives outside of school. They're not even sure we're human, which is why we suddenly become famous in the supermarket! They seem to think we live at school and survive on school lunches! So, it's important to show a bit of our "real" selves to them.

Here are two simple ways to become more "real" to your students:

1. Display an "All About Me" poster on the wall. Make it an entire bulletin board if you'd like. Post a few pictures of your family (No bikinis or Speedos at the beach, please!) or list a few things you like to do, hobbies you have, etc. Display an award you've received or a copy of your diploma.

2. Tell them stories about yourself. Students love stories, and stories make us seem more like real people with real lives.

Once you're seen as "real" by your students, they behave and perform better, if for no other reason than the fact that you're a "real" person who cares about them, and they don't want to disappoint you!

> "Once you are real you can't become unreal again. It lasts for always."
> — Margery Williams Bianco, *The Velveteen Rabbit*

47

Keep Your *Outside* Struggles Outside of the Classroom

What to Do

It's no secret that the teacher sets the mood, the tone, and the overall dynamics of the classroom every day. It's also no secret that teachers have real-life struggles that exist outside of the classroom. That's why it's vital that teachers commit to separating the two—their "outside of the classroom" lives from their "inside of the classroom" lives, especially when it involves anything negative or difficult. Easy? No. Necessary? Definitely.

How and Why to Do It

Let's face it: You're a real teacher who is a real person with real struggles. Maybe you're going through a tough break-up in your life right now. Maybe you have a sick loved one at home about whom you are worried. Maybe you had to referee an argument between your kids while you were trying to get ready for school this morning. Maybe you woke with an annoying, dull headache. These are real issues that you'll occasionally face. But it's important to keep your *outside* struggles outside of your classroom.

Students have their own lives and their own problems, so they certainly should not have the additional responsibility of taking on ours. We've all known those teachers who take their personal moods out on their students. The students *always* cause problems in those classrooms because those teachers poison the atmosphere.

There are two ways to ensure that you will never take your negative moods or personal problems out on your students:

1. Remind yourself that your students have their own struggles and they need your best every day, not just on the days when it's easy to be positive.
2. Be aware of the importance of smiling and faking a good mood, even though you're not feeling it. (See Tip 35.)

If you're having a day that is so bad that you cannot possibly fake it (and that day will eventually come), it's usually safest not to come to school on that day.

48

Ignore the Little Things

What to Do

In any classroom, on any day, there are lots of little behaviors that are less than perfect. If you address all of these little aggravations, two things will happen: 1) You'll have little time to teach, and 2) You'll fuel even more of these types of behaviors. However, you can defuse most of these by simply ignoring them. We'll show you how.

How and Why to Do It

If a student is tapping a pencil on his desk, he is rarely doing it inadvertently. He's trying to get a reaction. If you react negatively, he's likely to continue the behavior. Maybe he'll stop now, but he'll do it again later, with a louder, more elaborate rhythm. He might do it only when your back is turned and stop when you turn toward him, daring you to prove that he was the culprit. Instead, try ignoring it. These types of behaviors tend to bother the teacher more than they do the rest of the students. However, if the students are distracted by it and complaining, simply talk to the drummer privately. Say

I hadn't even noticed it because I like music and rhythm, but I need for everyone to be able to concentrate. Here's a trick for you: Try drumming with your fingers on your legs and it won't make a noise. I do that sometimes too.

Do you see what you've done? You've taken the "fun" out of it because you're not bothered by his behavior. You're even helping him to continue the harmless behavior in a more silent way.

Here are a few other typical behaviors that can usually be ignored:

- ◆ students slouching in their desks
- ◆ students mumbling under their breath after you ask them to get busy doing their work
- ◆ eye rolls from students or angry looks
- ◆ a student making funny noises (well, not funny to you...)
- ◆ an occasional quick side conversation between two students
- ◆ a bit of laughter between two students over an inside joke.

We could name a hundred more, but the point is that many behaviors are harmless and will disappear once the students learn that you're not bothered by them. And even if you *are* bothered by them, pretend that you're not.

49

Meet with Students Individually

What to Do

Almost all of our time spent with our students is spent with the entire group. We work diligently to differentiate instruction and provide individualized attention to each. But there's one step—a crucial step—that we often forget to take. We forget to meet with each student privately. Or maybe we don't actually forget, but we simply don't have the time. We'll show you a way to meet with every student and provide individualized feedback to each without taking any extra time out of your day.

How and Why to Do It

The meetings we are recommending take about two minutes each, and you can have each meeting during class time while students are busy on an independent (or possibly group) activity. Here's how: If you schedule two a day, per class—for two minutes—and if you have a class of 30, you can meet with everyone once in roughly three weeks.

Maybe do this a couple of times throughout the year. Even if you do it only once, it's better than not doing it at all. Make it seem official by telling students in advance that you will be meeting with each to *give* them feedback and to *get* feedback from them. You might even post a schedule of who you will meet with each day. At the secondary level where you have four, five, or six classes of 30, you may want to keep a private chart or make a note in your grade book in order to include everyone in the cycle.

Here's a sample of a quick individual student meeting:

◆ Identify an area of strength to let the student know you notice it.

◆ Identify an area of weakness and tell how you will help the student to improve.

◆ Allow the student to ask you questions or give you feedback.

◆ End by telling the student that you enjoy teaching him/her and will continue to do your best to help him/her succeed.

That's it. Simple and to the point. It takes only a couple of minutes, and it gives every student a very important message: *My teacher notices me, cares about me, is willing to help me to be my best self, and enjoys teaching me.* Any student convinced of that will work harder, behave better, and feel as though they matter more.

50

Brag About Your Students[*]

What to Do

Do you want student behavior to improve? Then brag about your students' good behavior to others—and do so in the presence of your students!

How and Why to Do It

This one is so easy. Whenever a visitor (parent, coworker, administrator, etc.) enters your room, use this as an opportunity to reinforce positive behavior by saying something like,

> This is the class I was bragging to you about. I am so proud of how they line up and quietly walk to the lunchroom each day. And, they are outstanding readers! Look at the list of books that they've read so far.

Hearing you brag about them to others helps cement a positive bond between your students and you. It also increases the likelihood that the desired behavior will continue.

Another approach is to tell your students that you were recently singing their praises. Say,

> I was bragging about you to the other science teachers yesterday, telling them that your biology projects were some of the best I've ever seen. I told them how attentive to detail you are and how well you work together to accomplish tasks.

You might also tell your class that you were bragging about them over the weekend to your family, the principal, or even the superintendent.

Remember that by treating students as if they are already the people you hope they become, you are increasing the chances that they actually become those people!

> Treat a kid as if you think he's better than he is,
> and he just might become a little better than he is.
> Act as though a kid is a whole lot nicer than he is,
> and he just might become a whole lot nicer than he is.
> Pretend to think a kid is a lot more helpful than he is,
> and he just might become a lot more helpful than he is.
> Act as though you know beyond a doubt all he'll
> achieve—
> because there simply is no stopping him once you
> help him to believe!

---

* This is adapted from Breaux and Whitaker, *50 Ways to Improve Student Behavior*, pp 102, 103.

51

Act Like a Recruiter

What to Do

What do college and professional sports recruiters do? They go out in search of players with talent. When they find those players, they do all they can to make them feel special, wanted, and needed. A recruiter aims to convince each player that the recruiter's team is the one on which the player will fit best and be the happiest and most productive. Today, we're going to show you how to "recruit" future students and make them think that your class is the place they want and need to be!

How and Why to Do It

In Tip 66, we'll show you how to teach like a great coach. But first, we want to show you how to recruit like a great recruiter. To clarify, we do realize that you don't have the luxury of selecting the students you want to teach next year. But if you act as though you do, the students will never be the wiser and your classroom will be the "team" they want to play for!

Here are *four simple ways to recruit students* to be in your class next year:

1. Talk to them in the hallways as you pass them or during lunch, recess, or bus duty.
2. Ask their names and introduce yourself to them.
3. Make an effort to smile at the students on the campus every day, because students will notice this and respond positively to it.
4. Stop at other teachers' classrooms when you're walking by and tell the students you hope they are in your class next year.

Also, if you're incorporating Tip 61, everyone already views you as the most professional teacher in the school, so you're ahead of the game. With a stellar reputation and by making an effort to make all students feel like your classroom is the place to be, you'll have students begging to be in your class next year. If they *want* to be there, that's half the battle! Put a copy of your Teacher's Creed (from Tip 56) on the wall outside of your classroom door. That creed, by itself, will do a lot of your recruiting for you! Treat future students like superstars and they're more likely to act like superstars when they join your team.

52

Let the Emojis Speak

What to Do

If you really want to know (and it's vital that you do know) how your students feel about you in general, let them tell you through emojis. We stole this idea from one of the most effective teachers we know.

How and Why to Do It

All students speak "emoji." Let's use that information to find out how they really feel about us. In Tip 7, we showed you how to elicit feedback from students about a lesson. In Tip 31, you received feedback about your teaching. Here, we'll show you one of the simplest ways to find out how your students really feel about you—all done through emojis.

Tell your students that because you're always trying to improve, it's important that you know how they feel about you. Assure them that this will be done anonymously, and ask for their honest responses. Then, give them the following emoji evaluation (Hand these out and then have a student collect them and leave them on your desk at the end of class.):

You may never get a truer picture (pun intended) of how your students view you than by giving them this short evaluation. Your goal, of course, it to get all of the left-hand column's emojis circled. If you don't, make it your mission!

53

Participate in Students' Lives

What to Do

Don't panic after reading the title. This one takes almost no time! Most teachers want to participate in after-school functions in order to show support for their students, but they simply can't find the time to do it. They've got families of their own and limited time to spend with them. The good news is that we have a trick for helping you to participate in students' lives without eating away at your precious time.

How and Why to Do It

So, there's a big football game Friday night. Most of your students and many of their parents will be attending. But you want to kick back with your own family because you've hardly seen them all week. Try this: Go to the football game for 10 minutes. Show up, walk around, and wave to as many people as you can. Be seen, then leave. The word gets out that you were there. And don't worry that you were seen leaving. On Monday, tell the students you had other plans but it was important for you to show your support, so you went and stayed as long as you could. Then ask who won. That's all it takes—showing interest! If you can't show up for the game, all is not lost. Simply ask about it on Monday.

In Tip 4, we suggested that you get to know one important thing about each student. This goes hand-in-hand with that, as you are letting students know that you're interested in what interests *them*. Most of the time, you can participate in their after-school lives without even showing up. If Tara let you know that she likes to dance and often competes on weekends, ask her about it. Find out when the next competition is. Mark it on your calendar and set a reminder for the day before. Wish her well the day before the competition and ask her how it went when she returns to school. This gesture goes a long way in showing students that they matter to you. And it usually takes almost no time at all!

Just in case it's too overwhelming for you to mark all of the students' events on your calendar, simply ask them to please remind you the day before an important event or activity occurs so that you can wish them well. You might be surprised at how many of them actually remember to remind you!

54

Be Available to Your Students

What to Do

We should never assume that our students (of any age) know that they can come to us if they need to talk or to vent or to bounce an idea or thought off of us. They need to hear those words from us, and they need to know they can trust us and confide in us if the need arises. So, take a minute to tell them just that.

How and Why to Do It

Will all of your students take you up on your offer to be available to them if they need to talk? Not likely. But it's important for them to know that they *can*. We've all had teachers who made us feel unwelcomed. We would have never gone to them for anything. Hopefully, we all had other teachers who were happy to make time for us if we needed help or if we just needed to talk. If students have a problem—school-related or not—they need to know that there are adults on the campus who *want* to help.

On occasion, it may happen that a student discloses something to you that you are bound, by law (and by good sense), to report. In this circumstance, tell the student that you have to report it—not only because it's your job but because you care and want to keep her safe. This does not make you appear untrustworthy. When students come to you to share that they are in danger, they actually expect you to help them, even if that means you must report what they told you to proper authorities.

Some students just don't feel comfortable coming to you to ask for help with a problem. They may not feel comfortable asking any adult for help. Or they simply do not know *how* to ask. In Tip 57, we'll show you how to give students an opportunity to share some of their challenges—without having to come to you to ask for help.

Sometimes, all students need is a listening ear. Often, a student will leave you saying, "Thanks so much for helping me to solve my problem." And you'll think, "But I didn't do anything. I just listened." Actually, you did a lot. You gave that student your time and attention. The student feels better, he sees himself as worthwhile, and he sees you as a hero!

55

Help Students to Set Personal Goals

What to Do

People who have goals, both short- and long-term ones, accomplish more than people who wander aimlessly. That's beyond obvious. Yet very few teachers ever take the time to help students establish goals—goals for the class and goals for their future. Today, you will simply be finding out what your students' dreams are. Dreams precede goals. You have to dream it before you can set goals to achieve it.

How and Why to Do It

Just to clarify, a dream is different than a wish. For example, "I wish my parents would let me do anything I want to and never punish me," is just that—a wish. Hopefully, it will never come true. But having a dream such as, "I'd like to become a veterinarian one day," is achievable. If you know that a student has that particular dream, you can encourage her and help her to start taking steps toward achieving small goals that can lead to realizing her dream—even if that student is a first-grader! She can begin reading about what veterinarians do, she can learn all about animals, she can visit a veterinarian and ask questions, etc. What's important is that you, as the teacher, do the following:

1. Ask students to share their dreams with you. From there, you can help them to set goals.
2. Have each student write two goals: What I hope to accomplish *in this class* and what I hope to do *with my life* one day. Keep a copy and have them make a second copy for themselves.
3. Occasionally, ask them about their goals and their plans to achieve those goals. Offer to help them in any way you can. But remember that sometimes the best help you can offer is to let them know you believe in them.

If you're concerned about finding time to do this, you can tie it into something you are already teaching. The key is to get them to write these goals. And since you will keep a copy, you can refer to them any time you feel a student needs a little extra encouragement or dose of motivation. Students who dream big and work toward goals are more focused, inspired, and hopeful. A classroom of goal-oriented, focused, motivated students? Yes, please!

56

Display a Teacher's Creed*

What to Do

One of the most effective things any teacher can do is to make a few promises to the students and then post those promises on the wall of the classroom. We'll share a sample Teacher's Creed. Feel free to use ours, or feel free to create your own.

How and Why to Do It

Here is an example of a Teacher's Creed—promises made and proudly displayed for all to see:

My Promises to You, My Students

I promise to be nice and smile often.
I promise to care about each of you.
I promise to be patient and understanding.
I promise to help you when you are struggling.
I promise to be fair and consistent.

I promise to be trustworthy.
I promise never to scream at you.
I promise to get to know you.
I promise to make learning interesting and
  meaningful.
I promise that I will not embarrass you in front of
  your peers.
I promise to challenge you to be your very best.
I promise to do all I can to help you succeed.
And I promise that, no matter what, I will never give
  up on you.

Rest assured that students will hold you to your promises. And also rest assured that if you stick to the simple promises of your creed, you will be the teacher that every student wants and deserves!

* This is adapted from Breaux and Whitaker, *Seven Simple Secrets*, p 111.

57

Make It Easy to Ask for Help

What to Do

This may be one of the simplest tips in the book. It merely involves giving students a one-sentence statement and allowing them to fill in the blank. Here's the statement:

"I think I could use some help with _____."

How and Why to Do It

As we mentioned in Tip 54, oftentimes, students are reluctant to come to you and ask for help, even though you've made it clear that you're available to them if they need your help. They may be struggling with something and would love to receive your help, guidance, or advice. But the thought of approaching an adult may be a bit daunting. Other students have no trouble at all asking for help. This activity is not designed for those students, but it includes them nonetheless.

Take a few minutes at the end of class one day and say something like the following:

> My main job is to help each of you to become your best self. None of us is perfect, and we all have things we need help with. Maybe you need help in class with a particular skill. Maybe you need help with a friendship that's not going well. Maybe you have trouble sitting still in class and you need some suggestions for what to do with your extra energy. It can be anything, school-related or not. Take a minute to think about one thing you feel you need help with the most, and write it in the blank. I'll collect these, read each one, and then I'll do my best to help you.

Then either hand them a slip of paper with the sentence "I think I could use some help with _____," or simply have them write the sentence on their own paper, fill in the blank, and hand it to you on their way out of class.

But what if a few students just leave theirs blank because they don't feel they need help with anything? That's fine. You're merely trying to provide anyone who needs your assistance with an opportunity to ask for it in a non-intimidating way.

58

Reinvent Yourself
Overnight!

What to Do

Teachers tend to be hard on themselves. They lament the mistakes they've made in the past and they often beat themselves up over those mistakes. Today, remind yourself that your past is who you *used to be*. Stop beating yourself up over it. You can reinvent yourself overnight and become more of the teacher that every student wants, needs, and deserves. That's not to suggest that you're not already an excellent teacher. But all effective teachers work diligently toward the same goal—becoming just a little better each day.

How and Why to Do It

Sure, we've all done things in class or said things to students that we instantly regretted saying or doing. None of us is perfect. Just as all effective teachers ensure that students start with a clean slate every day, it's time to remind yourself that you, too, can start with a clean slate every day. In this tip, we'll show you how you can reinvent yourself instantly, letting your past be just that—your past.

Let's say that you've gotten lax in appearing enthusiastic and positive on a daily basis. You may even have become a little negative in your thinking in general. The students, of course, notice this because students notice *everything*. Is it ever too late to change? Not in the classroom, it's not. Actually, the easiest place to reinvent yourself is in the classroom. Do you know why? Because students will believe you're a changed person if you exhibit a new behavior for only a few days. Students are young, innocent, and trusting. And no matter how negative you may currently be, if you exhibit a positive demeanor for a few consecutive days, they'll *buy it*. They'll believe you are a changed person. The first day of revealing the new-and-improved you, you'll see shock on their faces. You may even be asked if something is wrong. By the second day, they're wondering if this really is a *new you*. And by day three, they're all in and grateful that you are now a new and improved positive role model.

Adults, on the other hand, are not nearly as quick to believe us when we display a new behavior. Go home and display the new and improved version of yourself. Every adult in the house will sleep with one eye open for the next six months! Thankfully, students are not so skeptical. Start every day in your classroom with a clean slate and work at becoming an even better version of yourself.

59

Let the Games Begin!

What to Do

No one will argue that the more fun something is, the more appealing it is. Therefore, it stands to reason that we want to do everything we can to "fun-up" our classrooms. The more fun your class is, the more the students look forward to it. The more fun you are, the better the students relate to you. The better your students relate to you, the more productive they are.

In Tip 40 we showed you a way to raise the fun level in your classroom by holding occasional raffles. Today, we'll show you how to raise the fun level at any time on any day by turning learning activities into games.

How and Why to Do It

You can make almost any task fun if you turn it into a game. And your games don't have to be fancy. Have you ever noticed that a toddler will often choose to bang a spoon on a pot rather than playing with the expensive, technologically-advanced toy you just spent a week's salary on?

Students of all ages (and even adults) love to play games. A quick online search for the term "classroom learning games" will practically overwhelm you with creative ideas for turning any activity into a learning game.

There are classroom versions of popular gameshows and old-school board games that students love to play—Jeopardy, Family Feud, Trivial Pursuit, Human Tic-Tac-Toe, Scrabble, Pictionary, and you name it. There are apps too numerous to list that provide games for just about anything you are teaching. There are even apps that turn questions and vocabulary words into a quiz show format. Best of all, they're free!

Here's an easy way to turn any test review into a game. Get some buzzers (or use a buzzer app) and divide the students into teams. Ask questions and have them compete to see who can buzz-in first with the correct answer. When you turn test reviews into competitive games, the students look forward to them and tend to prepare better for the test! And when your classroom is a fun place to be, the students look forward to coming to it every day. Let the games begin and everyone will win!

60

Tell Students You Don't Hold Grudges

What to Do

Even if you're a person who never holds grudges, the students will not know this unless you tell them. If you *are* a person who holds onto things a little too long, *still* tell the students you don't hold grudges. Then fake it and act as though you truly do let things go quickly.

How and Why to Do It

Students do not like feeling that their past actions are being held over them. They can become resentful, defensive, and mistrusting of the person who is holding a past action over them. Resentful, defensive, mistrusting students invariably become behavior problems. They also learn to hold grudges themselves.

In our classrooms, our students need to be assured that every day is a new day. The past is the past, and it is over. And they need to be reassured that their teachers are mature adults who do not hold the past over their heads.

Let's say that a couple of students get caught cheating on a test. There is a consequence attached. They know that you are disappointed in them. And they may think you will now hold this against them. Explain that you wipe the slate clean every day. We all make mistakes and occasional bad decisions. What's important is that we learn from these mistakes and do better going forward.

It's difficult to move forward if the people around you continue to be upset about what you did in the past. Tell your students that you have "selective amnesia." You remember everything they do that is *good* and forget everything they do that is *not good*. Saying this once is not enough, but at least it sets the stage. You'll need to continue to convince them, through your words and, most importantly, your actions, that you do not hold grudges and that you give everyone a fresh start every day.

After a student does something that warrants a consequence or reprimand, be sure to remind the student that it's over now. "Let's learn from it, and let's use what we've learned to make better choices next time." Then smile and say, "Can't wait to see you tomorrow!"

61

Be the Most Professional Teacher in the School

What to Do

Every teacher, in every school, has a reputation. A positive reputation is vital to your success as a teacher and your relationships with your students. A negative reputation is poisonous. Simply put, there's no downside to having a positive reputation and no upside to having a negative one. The easiest way to establish and maintain a positive reputation is to be (or at least act as though you are) the most professional teacher in the school. We'll show you how.

How and Why to Do It

To begin with, you may want to refer back to Tip 58 where we discussed how to leave the past behind and reinvent yourself, overnight, if necessary. If you've participated in less-than-professional behaviors in the past, so be it. Starting today, you need only commit to a few simple behaviors that will soon resurrect your good reputation and catapult you to the height of professionalism.

Seven Simple Ways to Be the Most Professional Teacher in the School

1. Speak well of others.
2. Speak positively *to* others.
3. Avoid the following poisons: gossiping, griping, and grimacing.
4. Be willing to change your thinking as you learn and grow.
5. Do what you know is right and best for students.
6. Be consistently confident, competent, and reliable.
7. Speak, dress, and act like a true professional. On days when you don't feel it, fake it.

If some of the behaviors in the list make you feel uncomfortable, simply flag those behaviors as areas *in need* of improvement and begin working *toward* that improvement. If you already have the most positive, professional reputation on the campus, do two things: Pat yourself on the back, and then commit to becoming even better than you already are! No teacher will ever risk being *too professional* or having a reputation that is just too darned good.

62

Teach Students *How* to Think, Not *What* to Think

What to Do

We all know the timeless adage, "Give a man a fish and you feed him for a day. Teach a man to fish and you feed him for a lifetime." Bringing that same philosophy into the classroom, Margaret Mead said, "Children must be taught *how to think, not what to think.*" It requires no extra time to teach a student *how* to think as opposed to *what* to think. It merely takes an awareness of the importance of doing so. Students thrive in classroom environments where they are encouraged to think for themselves.

How and Why to Do It

Consider that if you give students a piece of knowledge, they now possess knowledge but don't necessarily understand what to do with that knowledge. If you teach them how to use what they know by thinking about it, analyzing it, solving problems with it, and creating with it, the possibilities of where that original knowledge can go are endless. As teachers, our main job is not to get students to think like we do. Our main job is to teach them to think for themselves. Students may know that 5 x 5 = 25. That's knowledge. But do they know what it means? Do they know that it means "5 times I see 5?" And do they know how to use multiplication skills to solve new problems?

We need to help students understand their own thought processes and then put them in situations where they are required to think for themselves. Here are some simple questions and prompts to help students think about their thinking:

◆ "How did you arrive at that conclusion?"
◆ "What changed your mind?"
◆ "Why?"
◆ "Can you walk me through your thought process when you came up with that story?"
◆ "How'd you come up with that fantastic idea?"
◆ "It's okay that you made that mistake. But let's analyze what you were thinking that led you to that mistake. We'll go through your thought processes for each step."

By teaching students *how* to think, we go beyond memorization of facts by feeding their curiosity and creativity. Once they know how to investigate, analyze, and use their thinking to solve problems, they can look beyond the obvious and discover what is possible. And now their plates will be full with the fish *they* have caught!

63

Make It Okay to Make a Mistake

What to Do

A high school coach shared a chant he uses with his players following mistakes or lost games: "It's over, it's done. Goodbye! It's gone. Learn a lesson from it, and let's move on."

Try a similar chant with your students, or at least teach them to embrace the philosophy of the chant by making it okay to make a mistake.

How and Why to Do It

In general, students hate to make mistakes. They often feel like failures when they make mistakes. Sometimes they get mad, sulk, or give up completely. "The correction marks on my test equate to bad grades, so how can this be a good thing?" Though we're not suggesting that you stop grading tests, we are suggesting that you help students understand that "red marks" (and mistakes in general) can present information and opportunity. Every time you make a mistake, you're presented with new opportunities. You can use the mistake to grow or wallow, to learn or stagnate, to stretch or recoil. The good news is that we get to choose how we *use* each mistake. But in so many classrooms, teachers forget to "teach" students that all mistakes can lead to growth, inspiration, and innovation.

Tell students the following:

> Don't let a mistake *beat* you up. Rather, let it *build* you up! Making a mistake enables you to become a better risk-taker and problem-solver. All smart, successful people take risks and are excellent problem-solvers. So, I actually welcome your mistakes and will often thank you for making them! In fact, your mistakes will help us all to become better thinkers, risk-takers, and problem-solvers.

You may want to tell them about a few famous mistakes in history: Penicillin, Silly Putty, Post-it Notes, the fact that windows on airplanes are now rounded as opposed to squared, the fact that the *Titanic* didn't have enough lifeboats because they thought it was unsinkable... Share some of your own mistakes and tell students how you learned and grew from those mistakes. "Hey, if the teacher makes mistakes, then I guess it's okay if we do, too."

Your approach to mistakes will be become *their* approach. Teach students to welcome mistakes and use them to solve problems. Make it *cool* to make a mistake in your class!

64

Tell What You Like About Each Student

What to Do

One day, when students enter your classroom, give them each a one-sentence note that says,

"Dear _____,

One of the many things I like about you is

_____."

How and Why to Do It

This simple note can have a profound influence on your students. Just print these and fill them in. If you worry that this will be time-consuming, here's a way to do it using no extra time at all. Begin filling these out a couple of weeks before handing them out. During class time, while you are walking around monitoring while students are working independently, fill out a few. Each should take no more than 30 seconds. You're walking around anyway, and you are in class anyway, so it takes zero extra time.

Notice that the note says, "One of the many things I like about you is _____." It doesn't say, "What I like about you is _____." There are two key parts to this: (1) The fact that you said "one of the many" as opposed to "one thing." This way, you're telling students that there are multiple things you like about them but are merely mentioning one here, and (2) The fact that you listed something specific that you like about each student. Here's an example:

"Dear Marly,

One of the many things I like about you is the fact that you're not afraid to ask for help when you need it. That takes courage and maturity!"

After all students have received their notes, ask them if you can post these on the student wall (see Tip 16) next to their pictures. Some will be anxious to have you post these. But if anyone doesn't want his/her picture to be posted, don't post it. Some may want to keep it so that they can post it in their bedrooms at home. But know that this simple note telling them you noticed something good in them will mean something special to each student who receives it. The more special the students feel, the more of their best you will receive!

65

Give Students the Benefit of the Doubt

What to Do

There's benefit to giving someone the benefit of the doubt—especially when that someone is a student. Today, we'll show you how to give students the benefit of the doubt, even if you *know better* and there is *no actual doubt...*

How and Why to Do It

How do you give someone the benefit of the doubt if there is no doubt? That's sort of an oxymoron, isn't it? Occasionally it happens that you know a student did something wrong. So, you're actually "pretending" to give her the benefit of the doubt when you say, "I know you didn't mean to hurt Sharla's feelings when you said that, but it did hurt her feelings, and I know you can understand why. Thanks, in advance, for apologizing to her." Do you see what happened? You just gave her a triple dose of the benefit of the doubt. You assumed she meant no harm, you assumed she understands why she hurt Sharla's feelings, and you assumed she will apologize. That's much more effective than saying, "Yes you did mean to hurt her feelings. Now go and apologize."

Sometimes, you suspect a student did or is about to do something wrong, but you're not sure. Act as though you believe the student's intentions are good. Let's say that you see a student getting out of his desk and you're almost certain that he is on his way to argue with another student. Say something like, "Wayne, I can tell you're on your way to help J.J. Thanks. I love to see you helping one another." Almost always, Wayne will do one of two things: 1) He'll turn around and go back to his seat, or 2) He'll actually help J.J.

Before the big assembly, try saying something like

I was just bragging to the other teachers about you. Some said they were worried that their students were going to talk during the assembly tomorrow. I told them that I wasn't worried about this class because I trust you to behave well. So now everyone will be watching us because I made you sort of famous. (See Tip 50 for more examples of "bragging" about them to others.)

In order to teach students, we have to reach them first. They need to know that we believe in them before they'll believe in us. And sometimes the best way to show that you believe in them is by giving them the benefit of the doubt, or at least pretending to!

66

Teach Like a Great Coach

What to Do

Great coaches and great teachers have more in common than most realize. With the exceptions of the arena and the content, there's not a whole lot of difference between great coaching and great teaching. Today, we'll be showing you how to teach for maximum effectiveness, just like all great coaches do—not good coaches, and definitely not bad coaches, but great coaches!

How and Why to Do It

Let's compare a great football coach to a great teacher to prove the similarities:

♦ Where is the coach during the game? Seated behind the desk? Nope. The coach is walking up and down the sideline, monitoring, calling plays, encouraging, and cheering the players on. Where is a great teacher during class? Seated behind the desk? Nope.

The teacher is walking around the room monitoring, guiding (calling plays), encouraging, and cheering the students on.

◆ How does a coach plan for a game? By writing a game plan—a very detailed plan with plays for the game along with many contingency plays for the "what if" moments of the game. How does a teacher plan for a lesson? By writing a lesson plan—a very detailed plan with activities for the lesson along with contingency plans for "what ifs."

◆ What does a coach do if the players are not succeeding during the game? The coach calls "time out" and re-teaches on the spot. What does a great teacher do if the students are not succeeding during the lesson? The teacher stops teaching (same as calling a "time out") and re-teaches on the spot.

◆ How many motivational speeches (pep talks) does a typical coach give during a game or even a practice? It's hard to know because the motivational speeches occur spontaneously and are ongoing. How many motivational speeches does a great teacher give during a lesson? It's hard to know because the motivational speeches (pep talks) occur spontaneously and are ongoing.

◆ How does a coach get the most out of all players? By convincing the players that they can do it and by helping those players to improve continually. How does a great teacher get the most out of all students? By convincing the students that they can do it and by helping those students to improve continually.

Point proven. Teach like a great coach and you will be a great teacher!

67

Give an Exit Ticket

What to Do

If you want to receive some instant, useful feedback (about how well the lesson objective was achieved, how the students did or did not enjoy an activity, or how well they understood a particular concept), or if you want to receive feedback from students about anything in general, give them an exit ticket. The possibilities are limitless.

How and Why to Do It

Exit tickets are free, quick, fun, and informative. They allow you to informally assess your students' understanding, feelings, and/or thinking about what they are learning in your classroom.

Here are a few questions and/or statements you might choose to include on an exit ticket:

♦ Tell two things you learned today.
♦ One thing I still don't understand is _____.

♦ Do (4 x 4) + 5 and 4 x (4 + 5) have the same answer? Explain.
♦ What was your favorite activity in class today? Why?
♦ What was your least favorite activity in class today? Why?
♦ Give two examples of physical changes and two of chemical changes.
♦ Use "their," "there," and "they're" correctly in the following sentence: _____ on the way to _____ car which is located over _____.
♦ Given the following weather conditions (list the conditions), predict the path of the hurricane on this tracking map.

A quick, online search for the term "student exit tickets" will yield countless samples of exit tickets, ideas for exit tickets, printable exit tickets, and even editable exit tickets for any age level and any subject area. The information gleaned from an exit ticket today can help you to be a more effective teacher tomorrow!

68

Control Your Body Language

What to Do

The science behind body language is undeniable—how you present yourself makes a substantial difference in how others perceive you. It also affects how you perceive yourself! The ability to control your body language is critical to your success in the classroom. We'll show you some simple ways exude confidence, competence, enthusiasm, and professionalism every day that you teach—all achieved by simply controlling your body language.

How and Why to Do It

The first step to controlling your body language is to be *aware* of it. Start noticing what you do with your body when you are happy (smiling), sad (drooping posture, falling facial muscles), excited (wide-eyed), bored (slouched, eyes closed, sleeping?), angry (clenched teeth, erratic breathing, red-faced), and so on. Though we don't all use the same body language to express the same emotions, our bodies can tell onlookers exactly what's going on inside our minds. One of the easiest ways to be aware of your body language in the classroom is to watch yourself on video, if you dare.

When dealing with students, follow a few *simple dos and don'ts of body language*:

- ◆ *Do* make eye contact when speaking with students, but *don't* use what we all know as a "teacher eye" that is meant to intimidate.
- ◆ *Do* control your voice, even and especially when upset, and speak calmly. *Don't* yell at students, as it tells them you are no longer in control.
- ◆ *Do* look as though you believe in and love what you are teaching. *Don't* ever appear tired, bored, or indifferent.
- ◆ *Don't* roll your eyes or slap your forehead with the palm of your hand.
- ◆ *Do* keep your shoulders back, smile a lot, and appear happy and confident. When sitting, don't slouch.
- ◆ *Do* appear serious, but calm and caring, when reprimanding a student, but *don't* appear angry as though you are taking the student's behavior personally.
- ◆ *Do* move around the room a lot, show interest in what students are doing, and be available to help them.

And lastly, *do* notice that the best teachers on the faculty always exhibit the most positive body language!

69

Determine the Origin of the Problem*

What to Do

Do you ever watch a student act inappropriately and then ask yourself, "Is it me?" We all know that the same students can act differently in different teachers' classrooms. And we also know that there are two types of problems in the classroom—student-related problems and teaching-related problems. Today, you'll learn how to determine if a particular problem in your classroom is student- or teacher-related.

How and Why to Do It

Before you can effectively deal with a problem, it's important to be able to diagnose the cause of the problem. And before you read further, we want you to know that it will be *good* news if you determine that a problem is teacher-related. If a student misbehaves because of something you are doing or not doing, that's good news because it's easy to fix *you*. It's not as easy to fix someone else.

Here's the simplest way to determine where the problem originated. Remember, you can't ever assume a problem is a *student* problem until all of the following are in place in your classroom: (1) Procedures are evident, (2) Organization is evident, (3) Positive rapport with students is evident, (4) The teacher appears enthusiastic, (5) There is no "down time" where students have nothing to do, (6) The teacher ensures success for all students, (7) Lessons are well-planned, relate to lives of students, and are engaging, (8) Every student is treated with dignity, and (9) The teacher does not allow students to push his or her buttons.

That's it. If you can answer "yes" to all of the list above, then the problem is student-related. If you can't— if even one of the nine is missing or lacking—then you'll have to work on that one area before you can determine if the problem is student-related. If you determine that a problem may be teacher-related, make a simple adjustment. If it's student-related, deal with the student.

In well-managed, well-organized classrooms where teachers have positive relationships with students and work to ensure that students are involved, engaged, and successful, behavior problems are minimal and are usually student-related.

---

* This tip is adapted from Breaux and Whitaker, *50 Ways to Improve Student Behavior*, pp 39–41.

70

Send One Note, Per Class, Per Day

What to Do

We'll preface this tip by saying that, at first glance, this may seem like something that will take *extra* time that you honestly don't have. It won't. We'll show you how to send one positive note, per class, per day to a parent or guardian. And we'll show you how to do it in under 30 seconds—during class time. If you have 30 students in a class and you send one note a day, then every parent will hear from you every six weeks or so.

How and Why to Do It

The first thing you'll want to do is print plenty of these— just a generic note with blanks to fill. Here's a sample:

Dear _____(parent guardian),

I'm so proud of _____(student) because _____(reason you're proud). I knew you'd be proud also.

_____(your signature)

Let's say that class begins and you notice that Ellen Thompson is busy working. Ellen doesn't always pay attention or do her work without encouragement from you. While you're walking around helping students, grab one of your ready-to-go notes and write: "Dear <u>Mrs. Thompson</u>, I'm so proud of <u>Ellen</u> because <u>she is working extra hard today</u>. I knew you'd be proud also." Then sign your name. Now immediately give the note to Ellen, give her a thumbs-up and a smile, and say, "This is for your mom."

It takes practically no time or effort to send one positive note per class every single day. Don't seal it in an envelope. Let the student see it. These types of messages almost always have a way of making it home and onto the refrigerator!

Keep the blank notes in a convenient spot on your desk. You might put a few in your pocket at the beginning of the day. You'll already be in class, so you won't have to "find time" to do this. You'll be walking around helping students or monitoring their current activity. Again, no extra time. And the results are nothing short of amazing. Teachers who send these notes home daily are much more likely to have better relationships with parents (and students) than teachers who don't. It's not rocket science. Do you want parents off your back and on your side? Send positive notes home!

71

Keep Students Engaged from Bell to Bell

What to Do

Most of us have made the mistake of saying this (or something similar) to our students: "Okay, we've finished the lesson and we have only a minute and a half until the bell rings. If you can keep quiet, I won't give you anything else to do." Invariably, chaos ensues, and we get frustrated and say that they "just won't listen" or they "just don't appreciate the fact that I tried to give them a bit of a break," or, "Kids today just take advantage of a good thing."

The truth of the matter is that kids will be kids. Any time you give students even a few seconds with nothing to do, they will find something to do—and it will almost never be what you had in mind! Lesson: Keep your students engaged from bell to bell!

How and Why to Do It

Effective teachers plan every minute of every day. They develop contingency plans for their contingency plans and seem to be ready for anything. But their biggest secret is that they plan for the *what ifs*: What if the lesson doesn't take as long as they planned? What if an assembly ends early and there is more time than anticipated when coming back to class? What if students finish an activity early? By maximizing time spent on instructional activities and being prepared for the "what ifs," they ensure that there is no "down time," meaning time where students have nothing to do.

When instructional time is structured and maximized and students remain involved and engaged, achievement improves and behavior improves because there just isn't any time for students to misbehave. They're too busy learning and having fun!

We are given a limited amount of time to spend with our students each day, and our task is to squeeze every drop of productivity out of the time we are given. The best way to do that is to plan for the "what ifs" and keep your students engaged, every day, from bell to bell!

72

Shake Things Up!

What to Do

Is it same old, same old when your students cross your threshold?
Because if it is, we guarantee that their brains will soon be growing mold.
So shake things up in a way that's controlled,
And watch their minds expand tenfold!

You guessed it: We're about to show you how to add some excitement to your classroom!

How and Why to Do It

If you've gotten into a rut and your daily teaching style is predictable and downright boring (even for *you*), then it's time to shake things up a bit. We all know that bored students either tune out, fall asleep, or get themselves into trouble. Yet some teachers are afraid to shake things up because they're afraid of losing control. The two are unrelated. You lose control for one of two reasons: (1) Your management plan is weak, or (2) Your lessons are dull and boring. You don't lose control by planning fun, unexpected, unpredictable types of activities that motivate and inspire students and spark their curiosity and sense of wonder.

So, do something unpredictable. Take the lesson outside. Change the seating by putting students in a circle today as you teach from the middle. Allow students to dress as a favorite character or famous person they are studying. Wear a costume yourself! Play a learning game (see Tip 59). Let a student teach a concept. Allow the students to teach each other (with your guidance, of course). It does not require a lot of effort to shake things up. It only requires a change of mindset.

By adding a little spice or excitement to the same things you are teaching anyway, it all becomes new, fun, and alluring! It doesn't cost a thing to shake things up a bit. But it costs a *lot* when students get bored—it costs precious time that can't be regained.

You can transform your classroom instantly by turning it into a place of wonder—a place that promotes curiosity, excitement, and inspiration, and a place to which students can't wait to come each day because they never know what to expect.

73

Thank Students for Being in Your Class

What to Do

Today's exercise could not be simpler. It involves thanking your students for being in your class. That's literally it—showing a little appreciation to your clients, your students. After all, they are the only reason you have a job.

How and Why to Do It

Before you begin class today, tell your students you have something you'd like to say to them. It will only take a minute, at most.

Here's a sample script for you:

I just wanted to take a minute to thank all of you for being in my class this year. Each and every one of you brings unique strengths and qualities to the class. If even one of you were missing, the class would not be the same. And all of you are the reason I have a job. I come to school each day because of you. And you make my job an absolute pleasure. I probably don't say it enough, but it's important to me that you know how much I appreciate every one of you.

That's it. A simple acknowledgment of how much you appreciate your students can go a long way in shaping how they perform in your class each day. When students feel appreciated, they work harder. That's just human nature.

Great teachers do this all the time. They recognize that students need to feel appreciated, and they take time to verbally thank their students.

You may be thinking, "But they didn't have a choice! They landed in my class because of the grade level and/or content area I teach." *You* know that, but *they* don't have to. Pretend that you hand-picked each of them to be in your class and that you are thankful every day that they allow you to be their teacher. There is *no* downside to showing appreciation. It's a well-known fact that gratitude affects attitude!

74

Call Every Student by Name, Every Day

What to Do

The simple act of calling students by their name on a daily basis gives them the very clear message that you notice them, you care about them, they're important to you, and they're special. So, it's important to begin calling every student by name at least once a day.

How and Why to Do It

There's actual science behind this: People (not just children) like to hear their names. They like to write their names. They like to see their names. They buy items with their names on them. They get excited when they see signs with their names on them. They enjoy meeting others with the same name as theirs. They put their initials on their license plates, their phone cases, their jewelry, their clothing, and on just about anything imaginable.

It's vital to get into the habit of calling every student by name at least once a day, but preferably more. Each time you speak to students, be sure to use their names. In your busy classroom, with so many students coming and going, it's easy to forget to do this. Therefore, you'll want to start making a conscious effort to say students' names as often as possible. For instance, Nate's hand is raised. You may be tempted to acknowledge him and say, "What do you need?" or "What's your question?" Notice that you did not speak his name. Instead, say, "What's your question, Nate?" Another example is a student providing a correct answer or doing something well. It's easy just to say, "Good job." But try saying, "Good job, Travis." You help to make students feel more important when you use their names. You cannot say their names often enough because no student can ever feel important enough.

But what if you have 120 students that come through your classroom doors every day? How will you remember to use everyone's name at least once every day? We'll share a quick, easy, fool-proof way for using your students' names at least twice a day without even giving it much thought: In Tip 9, we discussed the importance of saying hello to your students as they walk in each day and saying goodbye when they leave. From now on, say, "Hi, Tamara" as she enters the room and, "Bye, Tamara" as she exits the room. Do this for all students every day and you have called them all by name at least twice! But do continue to use Tamara's name each time you converse with her. It matters to show her that *she* matters!

75

Channel Your Favorite Teacher

What to Do

It's no mistake that we saved this one for last. It may possibly be the easiest thing you will ever do that will have the most positive impact on your effectiveness. All you need to do is think of your favorite teacher and then begin to act like your favorite teacher.

How and Why to Do It

We all had one—that teacher who impacted our lives more than any other: The one we will never forget. Get that person in your mind and just remember being in his or her class.

When asked to list *qualities of their favorite teachers*, most teachers have a remarkably similar list:

♦ was positive
♦ was kind
♦ was helpful

- ◆ made me feel special
- ◆ made learning fun
- ◆ didn't embarrass me
- ◆ inspired me
- ◆ taught me to believe in myself
- ◆ loved teaching
- ◆ loved students.

We're certain you could add a lot more, but the qualities we just mentioned are present in almost everyone's list. After all, who wouldn't love a teacher who was nice, made learning fun, inspired students, and was helpful and loving? All teachers want to be remembered fondly by their students, and to be remembered as a student's *favorite teacher* is just about the best feeling any teacher will ever know. So, on those days when you aren't quite sure how to handle a student or a situation in your classroom, simply channel your favorite teacher and handle the situation like you think your favorite teacher would have handled it. It's so simple and it's practically fool-proof.

If your students were asked to list your qualities as their teacher, would their list look like the one we just shared? If not, it's not too late. Revisit Tip 58 and reinvent yourself tomorrow. Your students deserve nothing less.

Conclusion

We hope you have enjoyed reading this book as much as we have enjoyed writing it. And we hope that you have found within its pages at least a few suggestions that have helped to make your daily classroom life more enjoyable, more productive, and less stressful. In deference to the hectic schedules we know you all keep, we did our utmost to make each tip simple and succinct.

Thank you, teachers, for all that you do. You have our deepest respect and admiration.

An Invitation for Your Comments

It has been our pleasure to share with you these 75 ways to be a better teacher tomorrow. We eagerly invite your input, your suggestions, or any stories you may wish to share for our future writings. Please feel free to contact us:

Annette Breaux: AnnetteLBreaux@yahoo.com
Twitter @AnnetteBreaux
Todd Whitaker: whitakertc@missouri.edu
Twitter @ToddWhitaker